SEIZE THE MOMENT:
NEW TESTAMENT DEVOTIONS FOR TODAY!

DR. JERRY D. INGALLS

All scripture references are from The New American Standard Bible: 1995 Update (La Habra, CA: The Lockman Foundation, 1995), unless otherwise noted.

ISBN: 978-1-955709-04-0

DEDICATION

I dedicate this book to the faithful congregation of First Baptist Church of New Castle, Indiana. Thank you for trusting God to call me as your pastor and for loving me and my growing family through these past twelve years together. We have been through so much and have grown closer to God, and to one another, because of our courage to persevere together in the unity of the Spirit, as the one body of Christ, for God's glory. Thank you, Jesus, for being so gracious and good to us! May the Lord bless us with many more good years of faithful gospel-ministry partnership.

Soli Deo Gloria!

CONTENTS

ACKNOWLEDGMENTS

I am blessed to be able to thank many people for the creation of this book. Preeminent to all is Jesus Christ, who teaches us in John 15:5, "I am the vine, you are the branches; he who abides in Me and I in him, he bears much fruit, for apart from Me you can do nothing."

Scott Underwood birthed the idea to respond to the COVID-19 pandemic with a daily phone call to the congregation. Scott worked with our business director, Tiffany Lee, to set up the Call Multiplier system, to facilitate this daily call for over 500 people. It didn't take long to realize I needed the assistance of my associate pastor, Pastor Ken Durham, who took responsibility for Saturdays, focusing on a hymn of the week. This allowed me to reprioritize a day of not producing content and return to a healthy rhythm of long-term pastoral ministry. Pastor Ken also created other special devotions for these calls periodically so that I could enjoy times of rest with my family.

Praise God for Ed Bell who suggested that we transform the existing content from the daily phone calls into videos that can be shared online. I want to thank Richard Kinnaird and Michael Dabrowski for prioritizing time every week to producing and posting videos of each devotion on our church's YouTube page. The videos from each devotion can be found on our church YouTube page, NewCastleFBC. Mr. Kinnaird has also faithfully posted the manuscripts of the devotional calls on our church's blog. The material found on the blog is the first form of this book and can be found at https://www.newcastlefbc.com/blog/.

Kimberly and the kids have lovingly adapted to this new rhythm of ministry that impacts them nearly every morning. They listen quietly and patiently as I record, and re-record (sometimes up to three to four times) the daily phone calls before breakfast every morning. My children's memories of their father in pastoral ministry will include these daily devotions and the intensity of pastoral ministry during the COVID-19 pandemic. I could not have done this without the prayers and support of my family—I love you!

Finally, this book is the work of a small team of committed people. While I take responsibility for all the content, and any errors found in this book, I am thankful for the editing skills, content suggestions, and book formatting of Emily Hurst and Sean Slagle. This book would not have been possible without either of them. Thank you for helping me get this content in a form that blesses not only our congregation, but many people beyond our immediate fellowship.

Thank you to the elders, leaders, staff, and congregation of First Baptist Church of New Castle, Indiana. Thank you to the over five hundred people that first listened to me nearly every day throughout the COVID-19 pandemic and to those who continue to listen to me as I continue this project by writing a devotion on every chapter of the Old Testament. Lord willing, you can anticipate the next installment of *Seize the Moment*, with a year's supply of Old Testament devotions, in late 2022.

> Praise God, from whom all blessings flow.
> Praise Him, all creatures here below.
> Praise Him above, ye heavenly host.
> Praise Father, Son, and Holy Ghost.
> Amen.

INTRODUCTION

Seize the Moment represents an intentional mindset for followers of Jesus Christ to strengthen their spiritual vitality and live on mission. Living in this mindset involves viewing every circumstance as a providential opportunity to grow closer to Jesus, as His yokefellow, and being aware of the Holy Spirit's promptings for faithful living. The method is simple—make time every day for the reading of a chapter of God's Word, followed by a focused meditation on an aspect of that chapter, concluding with an invitation to prayerfully apply God's Word in your day, for His glory.

Seize the Moment is for any follower of Jesus Christ. I wrote these devotions while pastoring a local church during the COVID-19 pandemic in an effort help my congregation stay focused on Jesus, and God's mission, through a time of great cultural disruption and personal unrest. While most of this material was written specifically for this project, some of it originated from a similar social media devotional initiative I did in the past. Every devotion in this book was written to be read out loud in under 2 minutes. These devotions are short and simple because I originally read them to the congregation through a daily phone call every day at 10 a.m. during the pandemic, starting in March 2020.

Seize the Moment is the product of real pastoral ministry! While I wrote every devotion in this book to comfort the congregation as we walked through this challenging time, I first received blessings from God through the daily process of writing them. I disciplined myself during the quarantine to rise early, read God's Word, pray through it, and then pray to God asking Him what would edify and encourage His people at such a time as this. My pastoral goals were the following:

1. Connect with the people every day and give them an open invitation to contact me personally for prayer or practical assistance during the pandemic.
2. Give the people a simple and short, but accurate and applicable, devotion from God's Word every day of the pandemic.
3. Encourage the people to stay in God's Word, to hear from God, and to live for God every day of the pandemic.
4. Equip the people to be hope-bearers and not doomsdayers in a dark time when the Church of Jesus Christ needed to shine brightly.

All these goals were met, but an unintended goal was achieved as well; my pastoral ministry was stabilized in a time of great upheaval, and my personal spiritual vitality was strengthened throughout a difficult time.

Seize the Moment can be used in different ways. The reader can work through it quickly or can choose to read one devotion per day over a year. While it is designed to be used as a daily devotional with your Bible, it also can be used by pastors, teachers, and leaders for a similar initiative in their churches, it can generate sermon-starter ideas for preaching through a book of the New Testament, or it can be fuel for group discussions based on the Bible. It is my conviction, through personal and pastoral experience, and from my doctoral research on how to strengthen the spiritual vitality of pastors, that the more regular and consistent you are with your daily devotions, the stronger your spiritual vitality will grow, regardless of the circumstances of your life or in your congregation.

God desires intimacy with each of us, so please approach this book as if you are hearing Jesus' personal invitation to take on His easy yoke and experience His light burden, not as a legalistic checklist of religious obligation. May you, the reader of this book, be daily blessed as you learn to find rest for your soul in the easy yoke of Jesus Christ (Matthew 11:28-30). This is my prayer for you, as it is my daily prayer for myself and for the congregation for whom I originally provided this devotional content.

MATTHEW

MATTHEW 1
GOD IS WITH US!

Have you ever felt alone? Have you experienced loneliness or isolation? Do you know what it is like to feel separated from your support network through difficult times?

There is good news: God desires for you to experience His presence through every storm and season of life! The Gospel of Matthew 1:23 uses these words to describe Jesus, "They shall call His name 'Immanuel,' which translated means, 'God with us.'"

Did you hear the truth of the gospel? God is with you! What a powerful promise!

One of my good friends, who is an intensive care unit nurse, shared with me the profound comfort this promise gives her. No matter the trauma or heartache of her daily experiences, she knows that God is with her. This is a promise she holds tightly: day after day, heartbreak after heartbreak.

This is a healing promise because, when nothing else makes sense in your life, you have the presence of God personally ministering to your heart and mind with His persevering peace. It is my prayer for you that the promise of Immanuel will comfort you and encourage you to keep walking faithfully.

The beautiful reality of this promise is that you have the security that, no matter the circumstances of your life, God is with you! Listen to Paul in Romans 8:38-39, "For I am convinced that neither death, nor life, nor angels, nor principalities, nor things present, nor things to come, nor powers, nor height, nor depth, nor any other created thing, will be able to separate us from the love of God, which is in Christ Jesus our Lord."

That is the good news of Jesus Christ!

Seize the moment and rest in the promises of God. Reach out to one person today to share this good news from God's Word!

MATTHEW 2
LIGHT IN DARK PLACES!

Matthew 2:10 highlights one of the details of the Christmas story, "When they saw the star, they rejoiced exceedingly with great joy." The story of Immanuel ("God with us") is the light of God piercing into the darkness of this world's situation and our human brokenness.

Jesus Christ is the light of the world, and He calls Christians to be the light of the world (see Matthew 5:14-16). Yes, the world is a dark place. Yes, our circumstances are challenging, if not scary. Yes, life is not always the way we hoped it to be. But, there is hope! As long as the sun rises in the East there is hope, because with the light comes hope.

God is not surprised by your current darkness, whatever it is. But, if we let it, the darkness can prevent us from being the light of the world. Don't let the darkness prevail—we are more than conquerors in Christ Jesus! Shine the light into the darkness. Reflect specifically today on how you can help others to see the light of God in the midst of all the darkness.

Seize the moment by being a hope-bearer, not a doomsdayer!

MATTHEW 3
BOLD, YET HUMBLE!

Matthew 3 focuses on John the Baptist, and I must admit that I am a huge fan! What a perfect guy to introduce Jesus to the world—bold with the truth and humble in his relationships.

John knew that his calling in life was to point people to Jesus, not to call them to himself. Therefore, he could be bold while also being humble. Humility is not thinking less of yourself; it is simply thinking about yourself less.

In Matthew 3:14, when Jesus approached John to be baptized, John's response was one of recognizing Jesus as the Lord. "I have need to be baptized by You, and do You come to me?" Jesus needed John to fulfill his life purpose through baptizing Him so that Jesus could fulfill His purpose in coming to earth. Wow!

God will use you in all of your circumstances, including the scary days, to point others to Jesus. God is taking that which the devil intended for evil and is using it for good!

Seize the moment! Be bold with the truth of God, yet humble enough to fulfill your purpose in this time, no matter the cost!

MATTHEW 4
FOLLOW JESUS!

In Matthew 4, we read the amazing account of how Jesus faced His wilderness experience and the temptations to give into His circumstances. Jesus was victorious and used God's Word to win the day! So can you!

In Matthew 4:19, Jesus invites with a promise: "Follow Me, and I will make you fishers of men [people]." This is Jesus' call to become His apprentice; He invites us to walk with Him on the Journey, through all that is happening today, and learn from Him as the Master Teacher.

Who are you following: Jesus or the world?

What is informing you: God's Word, social media, or network news?

Jesus' promise is fulfilled through the work of the Holy Spirit, in and through you. God's desire is for you to trust the work of God's grace *in* you to do the impossible *through* you.

May your prayer today be one of a willingness to follow!

Pray this prayer: "God, I ask You to fulfill in me what You began in faith. I believe that You can do this, and I come to You now with all of the heavy burdens and weariness of this day. I find rest in Your sovereignty and sufficiency. Please O Lord, rescue me and use me for Your glory. In Jesus' name. Amen."

Seize the moment and let God use you today, as you trust the Holy Spirit's power and presence to show the world Jesus in and through you.

MATTHEW 5
SEIZE THE MOMENT!

The days may feel dark and the news gloomy, but let us learn to "Seize the Moment" and not lose perspective. This too shall pass.

Seize the moment to love God and to love people!

In Matthew 5:13-16, Jesus teaches His people: "You are the salt of the earth," and, "You are the light of the world." You are God's plan to show the world God's love and compassion. Jesus is calling us to be a different kind of people by giving our life a new purpose!

How will you be salt and light to at least one person today?

Please don't allow yourself to get paralyzed by the news, or let fear, anger, anxiety, or any such emotion get the last word. Instead, make a choice right now to invest your time wisely, and choose to "Seize the Moment" as a divine opportunity.

Remember, the Church of Jesus Christ can never be closed because we are the Church!

Please pray today, "Jesus, my life has been disrupted. I cast all my fear and anxiety on You, and I ask You: how do YOU want me to be the Church today? In Jesus' name. Amen."

Seize the moment and be open to His still quiet voice and His providential opportunities.

MATTHEW 6
PRAYER IS ABOUT RELATIONSHIP!

There are lots of things around us that could cause us to worry about tomorrow, but Jesus says in Matthew 6:34, "So do not worry about tomorrow, for tomorrow will care for itself. Each day has enough trouble of its own."

Isn't that a truth we all need to hear? It's simple to agree with, but not easy to live (almost superhuman, especially in today's world). I am not inviting you to experience guilt if you are worried or anxious. No! Rather, I am inviting you to the heart of Jesus' ministry and teaching: Jesus is inviting each of us to a grace-paced life with His Father—into a vital, life-giving relationship, day by day, moment by moment. Jesus is inviting you to walk with Him on a daily journey that has no ending!

In Matthew 6:9-13, Jesus teaches us how to experience the heartbeat of this relationship with God! Join with me in the prayer He taught us to pray:

Our Father who is in heaven, Hallowed be Your name. Your kingdom come. Your will be done, on earth as it is in heaven. Give us this day our daily bread. And forgive us our debts, as we also forgive our debtors. And do not lead us into temptation, but deliver us from evil. For Yours is the kingdom and the power and the glory forever. Amen.

Seize the moment! God doesn't want you to walk alone through this time, so why don't you consider starting an ongoing conversation with Him right now? Is there someone you can invite to join you along the way?

MATTHEW 7
SHINE BRIGHT IN THIS DARK NIGHT!

Years ago, we were tent camping in the Badlands. The night sky was captivating! I was overwhelmed with wonder at the vast multitude of individual lights that were piercing the darkness of that pitch black night. It was a holy moment that changed my focus in an instant.

I learned that the darker it gets, the brighter the stars shine!

Many of us are scared, disappointed, and overwhelmed, right now. That is real and there is no denying it. In these times, it is easier to stay in the comfort and safety of our "tent" because it is cold and dark out there. But there is something waiting to captivate us and change our focus in an instant: It is the awe-inspiring love of God!

Just as a vast multitude of individual lights pierce the darkness of the pitch-black night, so God's love pierces the darkness of our current world situation when we, a vast multitude of individual lights, proclaim God's love in practical ways.

How?

Jesus invites us in Matthew 7:12, "In everything, treat people the same way you want them to treat you, for this is the Law and the Prophets." And you thought your mother made the Golden Rule up all by herself.

You are called to be one of the lights that pierces the darkness. But you have to get out of your "tent" to shine the love of God to another person. Yes, it is really dark out there, but trust me: The darker it gets, the brighter the stars shine!

Seize the moment: Shine! God loves you with an everlasting love.

MATTHEW 8
OUTCASTS, OUTLAWS AND IN-LAWS!

This is the Day the Lord has made, let us REJOICE and be GLAD in it.

Have you ever heard my joke about in-laws and outlaws? It'll make you laugh, or grimace: What's the difference between an in-law and an outlaw? The outlaw is *wanted*!

Jesus loves with the perfect love of His Father in Heaven. Matthew 8 is a dramatic chapter, on purpose, because it is the illustration of Jesus' Sermon on the Mount (Matthew 5-7). Like any good teacher, Jesus demonstrated His teaching with real life illustrations.

Jesus heals a leper who, back in the day, was an outcast of society (3). They were "social-distanced" to the max, but Jesus met his human need by touching and healing him. SCANDAL!

Then you have the Centurion, one of the enforcers of the Roman oppression of the Jewish people. Jesus not only heals the Centurion's servant, but Jesus praises the Roman's faith (5-13). Salt in the wound of the scandal!

Then, Jesus heals Peter's mother-in-law (15) ... WHAT!?! Does God's love know no boundaries!?!

(It doesn't!)

To drive home the illustration: Matthew 8 ends with the healing of Legion, which, by the way, got Jesus kicked out of town (28-34)!

God's love has no boundaries! How about your love?

Seize the moment: Reach out to an outcast, an outlaw, or an in-law, today. We all need love! And you never know how one act of kindness can make a difference in someone's life!

*Note from the author: I love my mother-in-law! She is a Joy to us!

MATTHEW 9
COMPASSION ACTS!

Being a parent can be very challenging and scary. When my first child was younger, he had night terrors. It was scary because we couldn't wake him up when he was having an episode. Oh, how we prayed because it felt like he was harassed and helpless! We prayed out loud over our son and we spoke lovingly and reassuringly to him knowing that our voices would help him through his dark and scary experience. We gave him a way home and we called upon the Good Shepherd to help him.

Matthew 9:36 narrates, "Seeing the people, [Jesus] felt compassion for them, because they were distressed and dispirited like sheep without a shepherd."

Jesus is the Good Shepherd; this is a title of intimacy, much like that of a parent to a child. A shepherd knows his sheep and cares for them personally. He leads and guides them to safety because he has compassion on them.

Compassion is like the love of a parent for a child in need. We wouldn't let our son go through his night terrors alone because compassion *acts*!

Seize the moment: Who do you feel compassion for? Pray for that person or situation, then act. Allow compassion to lead you to where the Good Shepherd needs you.

MATTHEW 10
FAITHFULNESS IN THE FACE OF FEAR!

Over 20 years ago I served in the Army as a paratrooper. A paratrooper's job is to jump out of an airplane in order to seize a foothold deep behind enemy lines, to help the Army win the war.

The Army's secret to a successful military jump is TRUST! Every paratrooper goes through rigorous training to learn to trust the jumpmaster, trust the training, and trust the equipment. To say that I got over the fear of jumping out of a perfectly good airplane and hitting the ground with the force of jumping out of a two-story window, with full combat gear, at night, is to miss the point of how the army trains its paratroopers—you learn to trust your jumpmaster, your training, and your equipment so much that you remain faithful in the face of fear!

It's the same now in my daily walk with Jesus; the key to successful Christian living is TRUST! Jesus taught us in Matthew 10:28, "Do not fear those who kill the body but are unable to kill the soul; but rather fear Him who is able to destroy both soul and body in hell."

I have learned that fear is real and the only way to be faithful in the face of it is to trust the Jumpmaster of my soul, His training, and His equipment—His Word and Spirit.

Until we learn to trust God with our lives and our death, and until that trust is worked deeply into us, fear will limit our ability to be faithful in the face of it.

Seize the moment: Start your day off with God every day. Pray and ask God to build your trust in Him. God has a mission for you: Are you ready to jump in?

MATTHEW 11
REST!

There I was, in the foothills of the Blue Ridge Mountains, outside of Dahlonega, Georgia. I was in the Army's highly coveted Ranger School. And to be perfectly honest, I was beat! For the first time in my life, I couldn't do it! To put it in the words of Jesus, "I was weary and heavy-burdened!" At the age of 22, those were the worst days of my early professional life. Looking back 23 years later, it was one of the most important experiences of my life.

In Matthew 11:28-30, Jesus Christ invites all of us who are at the end of our own power, "Come to Me, all who are weary and heavy-laden, and I will give you rest. Take My yoke upon you and learn from Me, for I am gentle and humble in heart, and you will find rest for your souls. For My yoke is easy and My burden is light."

Have you realized yet that you can't control the world at large, or the people around you, not to mention your own world? I truly hope so because the greatest gift I can give you today is the invitation to surrender control and to find rest for your soul. How? By answering Jesus' invitation to enter into a personal relationship with God through Him! It's freedom! It's rest!

Seize the moment: Take a break from social media and network news today, from your need to know all about it, and find rest for your soul with the One who does know all about it.

MATTHEW 12
STAND UNITED!

Two qualities I value highly in a person are integrity and loyalty. Integrity speaks to the unity within yourself, and loyalty speaks to the unity without, towards others. We see them both in Jesus and He is our rock on which we build everything else!

Jesus said in Matthew 12:25, "Any kingdom divided against itself is laid waste; and any city or house divided against itself will not stand." He was talking to religious leaders who were accusing Jesus of using evil forces to do His miracles. It's amazing how people can turn against each other! We have seen plenty of these days and not just because of the COVID-19 pandemic. The new American pastime is to divide against each other!

My hope and prayer for you and your life is that you will be united with Christ and, through His work in your heart and mind, you will use your words and time to build unity. That starts by being unified within yourself. That is your personal integrity. This comes through a personal relationship with God, where you walk and talk with Jesus and learn how to be gentle and humble in heart (also known as unity with God). Unity with God leads to loyalty in relationships.

Seize the moment: A house divided will not withstand the storms we face! Everyone has opinions, those are easy! Not everyone has integrity; that is hard! Reach out to someone today to build a unified house. Let's build on the rock of Jesus Christ!

MATTHEW 13
LET US PRAY!

As I was praying through Matthew 13, the Parable of the Sower and the Seed, I asked God what He would have me say to you, I felt in my spirit that God wanted us to spend our time together today in prayer. There is power in praying God's Word!

Pray this prayer inspired by the Word of God from today's reading:

Lord Jesus, we pray that the good seeds of the Word of God will grow in our minds and hearts, a great faith that prevails over all evil and perseveres through dark days. Your Word promises us that no weapon formed against us will prosper! Holy Spirit, activate within each and every person the faith to face this day and every day called today. May Your grace be our sufficiency. In our weakness, may we be strong because You fill our cup to overflowing with Your power and Your presence. Shalom! May Your peace, that is above all human understanding, guard our hearts and minds in Christ Jesus, as You walk with us through the valley of the shadow. May Your perfect love drive out all fear for You are with us, Your rod and Your staff they comfort us. May the joy of Your salvation be our strength as we learn to keep our eyes on You, the author and perfecter of our faith, Jesus Christ, the light of the world. Now and always. In Jesus' mighty and triumphant name we pray. Amen.

Seize the moment: The Word of God will not return void. Pray the Word of God. Pray without ceasing; pray the power and authority available to us through the shed blood of Jesus Christ.

MATTHEW 14
GO TO A SOLITARY PLACE!

Watch Jesus in Matthew 14:13a, "Now when Jesus heard about John, He withdrew from there in a boat to a secluded place by Himself." John the Baptist had just been unjustly executed by King Herod. Jesus took time alone to grieve, to be with God.

Are you grieving right now? Exhausted and worn with a constant barrage of feeds and needs pressing on you? The emotional weight of this moment is heavy. There is a persistent grief in this time that I have to continually bring to the Lord.

Jesus prioritized time for prayer. Jesus made this a pattern of His life; He sought His Father in prayer in solitude, apart from the opinions of people and the onslaught of demands. This is an essential rhythm of life that must be prioritized and protected, or it won't happen. This is one of the rhythms of the easy yoke of Jesus, a lifestyle pattern of Jesus' grace-paced life.

Seize the moment to slow down and find your value and worth, not in productivity, but in relationship with the God who loves you and desires to draw close to you. He is inviting you to "Cease striving and know that I am God" (Psalm 46:10).

MATTHEW 15
THE MIRACLE OF MULTIPLICATION!

Listen to Jesus speak to His disciples in Matthew 15:32, "I feel compassion for the people, because they have remained with Me now three days and have nothing to eat; and I do not want to send them away hungry, for they might faint on the way."

Are you ready to collapse from the stress and anxiety, confusion, and grieving in your life right now?

Are you hungry? Physically, emotionally, spiritually, relationally?

In His compassion, Jesus asked His disciples to give of what they had to meet the needs of the crowd (33-36). Jesus miraculously multiplied the little they had to meet all the needs, to the point of every person being "satisfied" (37-39).

Jesus' compassion invites us to help meet the needs of today. The Lord is with each of us and has called all of us to work together. Are you ready to bring what you have to the Lord and see how He will multiply it for God's glory?

Seize the moment by making yourself available to help another person with what you have. You'll only experience the miracle of multiplication by opening up your heart and hands!

MATTHEW 16
HEALTHY RELATIONSHIPS REQUIRE SACRIFICE!

Do you ever struggle with understanding Jesus' words and how to apply those teachings in the everyday ways of your life?

There is nothing more everyday than our relationships!

Cultivating healthy relationships over time can be very challenging and requires a lot of maturity to experience long-term satisfaction with the person and increased sanctification with God. In other words, it's hard work to have relationships that are both whole and holy, and are pleasing now and for eternity!

In Matthew 16:25-26, Jesus teaches us the key to success: "For whoever wishes to save his life will lose it, but whoever loses his life for My sake will find it. For what will it profit a man if he gains the whole world and forfeits his soul? Or what will a man give in exchange for his soul?"

Following Jesus and engaging in healthy relationships have a lot in common. Both require a willingness to put aside self-interest and an egocentric lifestyle for the sake of right relationships.

I also believe this is the way of the Church in how we are to serve our communities and the nations. Our witness to the world is dependent on not only our holiness unto God, but also our wholeness toward one another.

Why would the world believe we are right with God if we can't be right with one another?

You can't love your neighbor as yourself until self is no longer the motive of your love. Are you living both a holy and whole life?

Seize the moment and love your neighbor today in a practical, sacrificial way that demonstrates your willingness to love others by putting your own self-interest aside for your neighbor's sake. This is the abundant life!

MATTHEW 17
A MUSTARD SEED OF FAITH!

I tried out for the Olympic Team twice—in 1996 and 2000. Sadly, I never got to the Olympics, but I came close once and I had some amazing experiences along the way. I learned how a little confidence in competition can go a long way. It's amazing how the body follows the mind, especially in stressful times. Confidence leads to a positive cycle of trust and freedom!

This rings true with faith and life. A little faith can change your life in unimaginable ways!

In Matthew 17:20-21, Jesus calls His followers to exercise even the smallest amount of faith. Jesus stated, "For truly I say to you, if you have the faith the size of a mustard seed, you will say to this mountain, 'Move from here to there,' and it will move; and nothing will be impossible to you."

Jesus also compared the life of faith with Him to a mustard seed earlier, in Matthew 13:32, "This is smaller than all other seeds, but when it is full grown, it is larger than the garden plants and becomes a tree, so that the birds of the air come and perch in its branches."

Seize the moment by exercising your faith in small ways and watch God do unexpected things in and through you. Watch God do the impossible! Watch your life become a place where others come and find rest from exhausting and stressful days. May we each learn to trust Jesus more and, in doing so, experience the freedom to love people in practical ways.

MATTHEW 18
FREEDOM THROUGH FORGIVENESS!

Many years ago, I had to learn in a very personal and costly way that forgiveness is central to the Christian life—the Lord asked me to contact a specific person and confess my sin against them and ask for their forgiveness. Yes, it was scary! Yes, it was humbling! But, more than any of that, it was liberating!

There is freedom through forgiveness!

Matthew 18 is filled with Jesus' teachings on forgiveness. Verse 22 says we are to forgive, "up to seventy times seven." Verse 33 says, "Should you not also have had mercy on your fellow slave, in the same way that I had mercy on you?" Finally, verse 35 lands the plane for us, "My heavenly Father will also do the same to you, if each of you does not forgive his brother from your heart."

At the heart of our relationship with God is the issue of forgiveness—both in acknowledging what Jesus has done for us and then, in response to God's costly love, in how we are to live toward one another. It is scary! It is humbling! But trust me when I tell you how freeing it is.

Don't let bitterness and resentment get the last word in your life. There is freedom through forgiveness!

Seize the moment and pray about your next step in being set free through forgiveness—of yourself and others. Just as Jesus taught us, we pray, "Forgive me of my sins as I forgive those who have sinned against me."

MATTHEW 19
BE LIKE A CHILD!

I must confess to you that one of the silver linings of this current dark storm is that I am working from home, so I get to be with my three children more than usual. LOVE IT! Earlier this week, I got to be there when Willow, our six-year-old, road her bike without training wheels. It was awesome to be there and to watch the pure JOY radiate from her whole body. That night for dinner, Willow got an extra scoop of ice cream for becoming a big kid that day! It was so good for my soul to be with her, to remember the joy of being a child!

In Matthew 19:14, Jesus, the Mighty Physician, gives us a treatment plan for our chronic and terminal adult condition, "Let the little children alone, and do not hinder them from coming to Me; for the kingdom of heaven belongs to such as these."

As I write this amid all that is happening in the world during the COVID-19 pandemic, I am going to simply tell you to take this teaching of Jesus literally and not overthink it.

Seize the moment and do something today that will cause you to come to Jesus like a child. If you are physically able, go outside and skip, play hopscotch, jump rope, or shoot some hoops. If you aren't physically able, maybe watch or read your favorite childhood cartoon. I promise you: It will be good for your soul. And you can get an extra scoop of ice cream tonight for doing it.

MATTHEW 20
THANK GOD FOR MOMS!

I learned a valuable lesson about moms when I was the principal of Sunnyvale Christian School in California. We had over 200 students, which meant that I had a lot of moms to deal with. I learned that moms are designed by God to protect and advocate for their children. As a principal, I had to learn how to wisely navigate this reality with truth and grace. I'm still alive, and most of my scars from those 5 years are the type you can't see. So, praise God, I consider that a win!

In Matthew 20:20-21, we read a conversation between a mom and Jesus about her two sons: "Then the mother of the sons of Zebedee came to Jesus with her sons, bowing down and making a request of Him. And He said to her, 'What do you wish?' She said to Him, 'Command that in Your kingdom these two sons of mine may sit one on Your right and one on Your left.'"

Great job mother of the sons of Zebedee! Moms, please keep protecting, supporting, and advocating for your kids. Pray God's richest blessings on them!

I love my mom! She's the best! Thank you, mom, for giving me life, protecting me, and for being my greatest supporter.

Seize the moment: Call your mom today and say, "Thank you!" Say a prayer for your mom and bless her. If your mom is no longer with us, say a prayer thanking God for her. And to all the moms out there: Thank you! You know what to do, get to praying for those kiddos of yours … we never get too old to need your love and support.

MATTHEW 21
WHEN FEAR WINS THE DAY!

Fear causes people to do and say hurtful things. Fear changes the chemistry of your brain as you go into survival mode. Faith keeps us calm and helps us make better decisions—ones that are righter and truer for long-term thriving. My advice, in the COVID-19 pandemic and beyond it, is unchanging: **Remain Calm and Pray! God is with us!**

In Matthew 21:9, we read this account of Jesus entering Jerusalem, to ultimately find Himself on the Cross, "The crowds going ahead of [Jesus], and those who followed, were shouting, 'Hosanna to the Son of David; Blessed is He who comes in the name of the LORD; Hosanna in the highest!'" That is how the people of Jerusalem greeted Jesus—with faith! Hosanna—God saves!

Now, listen to those same people days later, after their fears had been agitated by local leadership. From Matthew 27:22-23, "Pilate said to them, 'Then what shall I do with Jesus who is called Christ?' They all said, 'Crucify Him!' And he said, 'Why, what evil has He done?' But they kept shouting all the more, saying, 'Crucify Him!'" Kill the One we thought was going to save us, but now threatens our way of life.

How do you react when you think something or someone is threatening your way of life or livelihood? Do you go on the attack and let your survival mode take over?

Seize the moment: Remain Calm and Pray! God is with us! Now is a time for God's people to be patient and trust the Lord! How can you practically help other people remain calm today?

MATTHEW 22
YOU BEAR THE IMAGE OF GOD!

Benjamin Franklin is quoted as saying, "But in this world nothing can be said to be certain, except death and taxes." In Matthew 22:21, we hear what Jesus said about paying taxes: "Render to Caesar the things that are Caesar's; and to God the things that are God's."

Did you know that, in this passage, Jesus is reminding all of his disciples that we are made in the image of God? It's no surprise that the largest US currency in circulation is the $100 bill, and guess whose image is on that: you got it—Benjamin Franklin—the death and taxes guy! Not so subtle, Caesar! So, go ahead and give the government back a bunch of those $100 bills, but never forget who you really belong to—you've been bought at a price, purchased through the shed blood of Jesus Christ on the Cross of Calvary!

I'm so glad Easter is always close to our tax deadline, because it helps me remember that for every believer there is a third certainty that is even bigger than death and taxes, and that is HOPE!

We have hope in the resurrection from the dead and hope in our citizenship in the New Heaven and New Earth. The price for both has already been paid in full! Thank you, Jesus!

Seize the moment and allow God to fill your account with HOPE. Remember, death and taxes don't get the final word, the God of all Hope does! How can you practically share God's hope with another person today?

MATTHEW 23
SHOULDERING ONE ANOTHER'S BURDENS!

Here is a true-story scene back from when I was training for the Olympics: I had a heavy load of 625 pounds on a squat bar pressing down on my body, and I was to do a full squat all by myself. But I had a "spot," which means I had a trainer behind me ready to support me under the weight if I were to get in trouble during the exercise. I was not alone!

In Matthew 23:4, Jesus contrasted the lifestyles of the religious leaders with himself, "They tie up heavy burdens and lay them on men's shoulders, but they themselves are unwilling to move them with so much as a finger."

There is one other place that Jesus used this specific word for heavy loads, and it is in Matthew 11:28-30, in His gracious invitation, "Come to Me, all who are weary and heavy-laden, and I will give you rest. Take My yoke upon you … For my yoke is easy and my burden is light."

Jesus invites you to a relationship with God that removes that crushing weight of religion and gives you a full-life, and full-person rest in the promises of God. Not because God removes the struggles and pains (the weights of this life), but because Jesus is now always there with you, doing more than spotting you, He is shouldering the load with you!

Seize the moment and don't even try to shoulder life on your own. Get in the easy yoke of Jesus and let Him shoulder it with you. Do you know of someone who could use some practical assistance this week? Let's do more than spot one another, let's shoulder one another's loads today!

MATTHEW 24
HOPE IN THE FACE OF SUFFERING

My wife is a rock star, for many reasons. I remember when Kimberly gave birth to each of our three children—natural childbirth with very little to no pain meds. I will never forget the intensity of what she went through as I held her hand, loved her through her suffering, and watched in awe and reverence the miraculous audacity that is childbirth. The full embodiment of pain, the waves of intensity, the sheer determination of creation to give birth to new life. I'll never forget.

In Matthew 24:8, Jesus summarized His teaching about the signs of the end times, "But all these things are merely the beginning of birth pangs."

Jesus tells us all these things in Matthew 24 to give us hope in the face of it all! Jesus tells us in advance so that we will not be surprised when life is more like a dystopian novel and less like a happily-ever-after Disney fairy tale.

Faith in Jesus allows us to go through the most painful of human experiences with hope! Let us look upon all that is happening in life with a victorious mindset, remembering that God is taking painful circumstances and making something beautiful out of them.

Creation is groaning. New life is coming. Hope in God, the Giver of all good gifts!

Seize the moment and keep your eyes fixed on the HOPE of new life that is being birthed through our times of pain and suffering! Consider sharing this message of hope with at least one other person today.

MATTHEW 25
STEWARDING YOUR LIFE!

At the heart of so much anxiety and unhappiness is comparison. We compare ourselves with what others have—their abilities, their resources or possessions, their jobs or service to the community … whatever!

This breeds anxiety and unhappiness because to compare yourself to another person is to miss the whole point!

In Matthew chapter 25:14-15, Jesus starts one of His most famous parables, "For [the Kingdom of Heaven] is just like a man about to go on a journey, who called his own slaves and entrusted to his possessions to them. To one he gave five talents, to another, two, and to another, one, each according to his own ability; and he went on his journey."

A primary lesson of Jesus' Parable of the Talents is that we are not owners of our lives, but stewards—household managers of what God has given us! You may have a five-talent life, or two, or one, but that is not the point, so don't make it the point! Stewards are not owners.

What you have isn't what should define you; those things are temporary. It's your relationship with the Giver that defines you; that is forever!

Seize the moment and steward the gift of your life well by growing in your relationship with Jesus! Learn from Him how to be generous with what God has given you. Don't compare yourself to others, but rather invest what you have into others. And watch the multiplication happen, along with peace and happiness too.

MATTHEW 26
A FOOL FOR JESUS!

I hate it when people judge my decisions or actions as foolish, but the opinions of others (which can so easily control me) can't be the measurement by which I determine my actions.

Matthew 26:6-10, tells the story of a woman who scandalously pours out her alabaster flask of very expensive ointment onto Jesus. Matthew tells us that everyone in the room, except the One, is upset by her "wasteful" display of worship. They all thought of her as the fool, except the One whose opinion actually mattered!

Jesus rebuked His disciples, and praised this woman, in verse 10, "Why do you bother the woman? For she has done a good deed to Me."

This perfume oil was worth over 300 denarii, which was nearly one year's income at the time. This was likely Mary's wedding dowry; she was trusting her future hopes of identity and security to Jesus alone—she was holding nothing back from Jesus.

Mary's faith led her to look foolish, but, knowing the end of the story, who was more foolish: Mary or Judas Iscariot, her loudest critic? Let's be careful about calling people fools until we know the whole story! Let's seek the opinion of the One who matters regarding our behavior and actions. Sometimes our loudest critics are the people we need to pray for the most.

Seize the moment and live for an audience of One. There is freedom and peace to be found in worshipping Jesus with all that you have. Hold nothing back from Him today. Are you willing to be called a fool for Jesus?

MATTHEW 27
THE POWER OF FAITH!

I write this as we are living in difficult and uncertain days! Each day, whether I feel like it or not, I get up early and I spend time with Jesus so that, through time with God in His Word and in prayer, I am strengthened to face the circumstances of this day through the power of faith.

Observe Jesus in Matthew 27:13-14, "Then Pilate said to [Jesus], 'Do You not hear how many things they testify against You?' And [Jesus] did not answer him with regard to even a single charge, so the governor was quite amazed."

The power of faith strengthens us to remain steadfast and resolute in God's plan for our lives, especially when our personal well-being and comforts are threatened, even to the point of death! Jesus did not give himself over to His circumstances or His feelings about them. Rather, He went to the Cross resolutely because He knew and trusted His Father's will for His life and death!

Most Christians have assumed that was easy for Jesus to do. We ignore the Bible's teaching that Jesus learned obedience through suffering (Hebrews 5:8). The Bible teaches us that Jesus would go off to lonely places to sacrificially invest time with God. We are called to do the same if we are to live like Jesus lived—with trust in God's will for our lives and our deaths.

The world tells you that your duty is to your heart, but your true duty is to God who speaks to you clearly through the Word and in prayer. Bring glory to God and find rest for your soul by living through the power of faith. Feelings are an important feedback loop in your life, but they are a fickle master. Trust God and build your life on the rock of Jesus!

Seize the moment and prioritize time to hear God's voice above your emotions and circumstances by spending time in God's Word and in prayer.

MATTHEW 28
PEOPLE OF THE RESURRECTION!

The reality is that living through uncertain times takes longer than any of us would prefer, but don't let yourself get distracted and emotionally hijacked by that. Trust this one thing: there is new life coming!

Listen to the resurrection of Jesus from Matthew 28:5-7,

The angel said to the women, "Do not be afraid; for I know that you are looking for Jesus who has been crucified. He is not here, for He has risen, just as He said. Come, see the place where He was lying. Go quickly and tell His disciples that He has risen from the dead; and behold, He is going ahead of you into Galilee, there you will see Him; behold, I have told you."

Do not be afraid; we are people of the resurrection! Our focus is not on the death, but on the life that comes from it. It is not on the disorder, but on the order; we are to bring to it. It is not on the brokenness, but on the healing work God has called us to do. We are people of the glorified King—Spirit-filled and born again into the living hope. We are people of the resurrection!

Now, go about your day remembering that death does not have the final word; disappointment in the fallen state of this world does not have the final word. Don't be afraid and don't despair, God is with us! Work as ambassadors of Jesus and His Good News—He is our Living Hope!

Seize the moment! New life is coming—anticipate it, lean into it, work toward it!

MARK

MARK 1
FIND A SOLITARY PLACE!

There is a difference between forced isolation and choosing to be with God alone. One brings life and the other death. There is a reason why solitary confinement is a severe punishment in prisons and why the silent treatment is a strangle hold on a child or spouse's well-being. Loneliness is a condition of your soul, and forced isolation is a poison to it.

Jesus pursued a solitary place with His Father. Mark 1:35 describes what I believe to be a reoccurring scene from Jesus' life, "In the early morning, while it was still dark, Jesus got up, left the house, and went away to a secluded place, and was praying there."

I know this is going to sound a bit upside down in days of social distancing, but please, the best thing you can do for yourself in times of loneliness is seek a solitary place to be alone with Jesus. Only God can heal your soul from the damaging effects of loneliness and forced isolation.

Seize the moment and make space and time for your relationship with God. Be careful about numbing yourself with TV or other "drugs" of choice. Those are false friends and will not provide you with the intimacy you need in this time. Run into the arms of Jesus by prioritizing a designated time, and a set apart place, to meet with Jesus every day. Use this time to create a new rhythm of life. Jesus is inviting you to come to Him and find healing and rest for your soul.

MARK 2
STRETCHER-BEARERS!

Last week, a small group of men from church helped a single mom and her kids move. Needless to say, in the middle of the COVID-19 pandemic, this took some hard work and creative thinking. We wore masks and gloves and, to the best of our abilities, kept our distance while moving heavy furniture down the stairs, through doorways … you know the drill. As one of the men told me afterwards, the gospel was proclaimed today.

Listen to Mark 2:2-4 as a small group of friends used both hard work and creative thinking to help their friend in his time of need:

And many were gathered together, so that there was no longer room, not even near the door; and [Jesus] was speaking the word to them. And they came, bringing to Him a paralytic, carried by four men. Being unable to get to Him because of the crowd, they removed the roof above Him; and when they had dug an opening, they let down the pallet on which the paralytic was lying.

Sometimes there are obstacles in our way when we want to help someone. Some of those obstacles are God-sized and require of us to pray and fast and wait upon the Lord. Other obstacles require us to do physical work and think creatively so that we can meet the need. We have to be willing to do either, whatever the situation requires of us.

Seize the moment and pray that God gives you the wisdom to know the difference. If it is time to wait on the Lord, then pray and fast for the person in their time of need. If it is time to get to work and be creative to find a solution, then be a stretcher-bearer for your friend and preach the gospel through your love and good works.

MARK 5
OPPORTUNITY IN DISAPPOINTMENT!

I like it when I get what I want. Who doesn't? But it is actually dangerous to always get what you want. How do you react when you are not allowed to have something you want? How do you handle disappointment?

In Mark 5, Jesus heals a demon-possessed man. The man then asked Jesus if he could follow Him. Listen to Jesus' response in Mark 5:19-20, "And He did not let him but He said to him, 'Go home to your people and report to them what great things the Lord has done for you, and how He had mercy on you.' And he went away and began to proclaim in Decapolis what great things Jesus had done for him; and everyone was amazed."

Denied! What did this man do after Jesus rejected his perfectly reasonable request?

Did the man throw a fit and demand his rights? Anger is a common response to denial, but sinning in our anger only makes a problem where there once was an opportunity for obedience.

Did the man throw a pity party, or become passive-aggressive? To devalue yourself or others is such a damaging response to disappointment, and it cuts you off from the moment of opportunity.

But the man did neither. Instead, he trusted Jesus' love for him. He obeyed Jesus instead of demanding his own way. God then used him to be the first witness to a people who had not yet heard of Jesus.

"And everyone was amazed" (20).

Seize the moment and trust God when you don't get what you want. Who are you when you are disappointed? Are people marveling at what Jesus is doing in and through you? There is an opportunity in every disappointment!

MARK 6
IN RHYTHM WITH THE CONDUCTOR!

I enjoy listening to music. One of the things I have learned about music is that rhythm is not just about what a musician does (playing notes), but also about what the musician doesn't do (pausing). In an orchestra, there is a conductor whose job is to "stress the musical pulse so that all the performers can follow the same metrical rhythm" (according to my Google search definition).

The same is true for our lives. In Mark 6, Jesus is at work "conducting" the disciples to both work and rest. He is teaching them to live a grace-paced life in His easy yoke, surrendered to the will of His Father so that they will work and rest to His glory. In verse 7, Jesus taught them to work by "[sending] them out in pairs, and [giving] them authority over the unclean spirits." In verse 31, Jesus commanded them to rest, inviting them to "Come away by yourselves to a secluded place and rest a while." Then, in verse 37, Jesus pulls them out of rest time saying, "You give them something to eat." Jesus calls them to work together and to rest together, but He also models the need for some alone time. In verse 46 we read, "After bidding them farewell, He left for the mountain to pray."

Are you in rhythm with the Conductor of your life? Are you focusing on His directions?

Seize the moment and get into a grace-paced rhythm with Jesus by focusing on Him as the great Conductor of your life. We live in a productivity-oriented culture, but you will be out of rhythm with your life if you are always hitting the next note instead of learning how and when to pause. Who or what is setting the rhythm of your life?

MARK 7
LIVING INSIDE-OUT!

When I was an athlete, we used to say, "Fake it 'til you make it!" Not feeling confident heading into a competition? Just fake it 'til you make it. Not amped up for a competition? Just listen to the right music and get the adrenaline going—muster it up, fake it 'til you make it. This was very much an outside-in approach to life.

Jesus teaches us a different way in Mark 7:14-15, "Listen to Me, all of you, and understand: there is nothing outside the man which can defile him if it goes into him; but the things which proceed out of the man are what defile the man."

Jesus doesn't want us to miss the point of life—the transformation of our souls to the glory of God. Jesus is not after us trying to be good boys and good girls conformed to the acceptable ways of the moral majority; He desires faithful disciples who follow Him in the narrow way.

Jesus is calling us to a new way of living, but not from the outside-in through worldly pride and performance, nor through religious conformity to rules and customs of man-made traditions. Jesus calls us to live from the inside-out, where our hearts are made clean by the grace of God and His character and good works flow out of us because we have become vessels of glory. Good works flow out of our hearts because God's Holy Spirit has made His home in us.

Seize the moment and take time today to pay attention to what is coming out of your heart—in your thoughts, words, and deeds—especially when you are put under pressure or facing hard circumstances. Often, it is our unplanned words and knee-jerk responses that will tell us the truth about our hearts.

MARK 8
A SECOND TOUCH!

As I write this, we have been under stay-at-home orders for over six weeks. Through this time, it has been my goal to be a messenger of faith, hope, and love to you personally while daily inviting you to seize the moment to make a positive difference in other people's lives. I know many people are getting tired and anxious for the next steps to begin.

Some things just take longer than expected. A classic story that illustrates this is when Jesus had to dramatically touch a man twice to restore his sight. It was shocking, because, in other situations, Jesus could just say the word and it was done. Watch Jesus touch the man for a second time in Mark 8:25, "Then again He laid His hands on his eyes; and he looked intently and was restored, and began to see everything clearly."

So often, there is more to the story than we know. We may never know, but that doesn't change our invitation to remain patient, persevere, and pray.

If you have ever been on a long airplane flight, then you know that what often feels like the longest part of an airplane ride is after you land and before you actually get to depart. Why? Impatience to get off and get going! Yes, it's been a long flight, but we are still in the air and, unfortunately, on this flight we don't know when the plane will even land or if the gate is ready for us yet.

Seize the moment: remain patient, persevere, and pray. Share this with people you know who are struggling with fatigue, anxiety, and grief.

MARK 9
GIVE A CUP OF WATER!

Friendships and healthy relationships are so important; in my opinion, they are what matter the most! Living at peace with God, and with your neighbor, is the recipe for good mental and emotional health. How does this happen?

Listen to Jesus' words from Mark 9:38-41,

John said to him, "Teacher, we saw someone casting out demons in Your name, and we tried to prevent him because he was not following us." But Jesus said, "Do not hinder him, for there is no one who will perform a miracle in My name, and be able soon afterward to speak evil of Me. For he who is not against us is for us. For whoever gives you a cup of water to drink because of your name as followers of Christ, truly I say to you, he will not lose his reward."

Living at peace with people happens by not drawing your boundary lines on who you can live at peace with too rigidly. Jesus seems to draw the line at the giving of a cup of water to drink. Where do you draw the line?

Too many Christians are drawing their lines on friendships and relationships based on politics and preferences that, honestly, say more about their citizenship on earth rather than their citizenship in Heaven. Ultimately, that says more about your relationship with God than it does anything else.

You always reflect the god you serve! Let's reflect to the world our peace with Jesus by demonstrating His love, care, and stewardship of His creation, one person at a time.

Seize the moment and learn to love your neighbor as yourself. How can you invest in healthy relationships today? Who are you going to give a cup of water to today?

MARK 10
MAKING THE IMPOSSIBLE POSSIBLE!

Have you ever tried to do something really big? So big, that people thought you were crazy? Maybe it was starting your own business, or taking on an assignment at school, or taking on a job that no one else was willing to try. Maybe it was loving a certain person that drives everyone else crazy. Whatever it may be, sometimes we are called to attempt the impossible.

When we do it for the glory of God, I think that brings a metaphorical smile to God's face.

In Mark 10, after calling a rich young man to do what was necessary to follow Him—to get rid of his false securities and fully trust God—the man walked away dejected because the assignment was too big for him. In response, the disciples of Jesus asked, "Then who can be saved?" It was culturally assumed in those ancient times that the rich had God's blessing already. But Jesus never made that assumption and He answered in Mark 10:27, "With people it is impossible, but not with God; for all things are possible with God."

Do you want to put a smile on God's face? Then trust God to do the impossible in and through you. Our own salvation is both impossible, because we can't save ourselves, and improbable, if we are honest with ourselves—we are saved only by the mercy of God. Why would our ability to do anything for God's glory be any different?

Seize the moment and step out in faith today. Maybe there is a neighbor you are supposed to help out today. If only the rich young man had taken steps to obey God, I believe God would have stood in the gap with him. I believe God will stand in the gap for you, too, because your decision to act in faith brings Him glory!

MARK 13
STAY ON GOD'S PLAN!

A story from my college athlete days: It was the 1996 NCAA Division I Track & Field Championships. I was in peak condition, and I was ready to compete at my highest level. But I made a mistake and I paid for it in spades. I let the overwhelming odds of competing against the Hungarian, who would become not only the NCAA Champion that day, but also the gold medalist in the 1996 Olympics a few months later, inside my head. I choked because I veered away from the plan. I allowed my circumstances to take control.

Christians are to remain hopeful in the face of what feels like overwhelming odds. When everything looks out of control, we are to walk by faith and not by sight. We are to stay on God's Plan as His Image Bearers! Reflect on Jesus' reassuring words from Mark 13:23, "But take heed; behold, I have told you everything in advance." and then, in verse 31, "Heaven [the skies] and earth will pass away, but My words will not pass away."

Be assured that, against all evidence presented by media outlets and from our own daily circumstances, the world is not out of control, but rather on a foreseen path towards the completion of all things. God has already told us so that we can remain focused! So that we can stick to the plan!

Seize the moment and remain faithful to God's plan. How are your responses to today's circumstances helping people see God's love and mercy? How are you stirring one another up to love and good works?

MARK 10
MAKING THE IMPOSSIBLE POSSIBLE!

Have you ever tried to do something really big? So big, that people thought you were crazy? Maybe it was starting your own business, or taking on an assignment at school, or taking on a job that no one else was willing to try. Maybe it was loving a certain person that drives everyone else crazy. Whatever it may be, sometimes we are called to attempt the impossible.

When we do it for the glory of God, I think that brings a metaphorical smile to God's face.

In Mark 10, after calling a rich young man to do what was necessary to follow Him—to get rid of his false securities and fully trust God—the man walked away dejected because the assignment was too big for him. In response, the disciples of Jesus asked, "Then who can be saved?" It was culturally assumed in those ancient times that the rich had God's blessing already. But Jesus never made that assumption and He answered in Mark 10:27, "With people it is impossible, but not with God; for all things are possible with God."

Do you want to put a smile on God's face? Then trust God to do the impossible in and through you. Our own salvation is both impossible, because we can't save ourselves, and improbable, if we are honest with ourselves—we are saved only by the mercy of God. Why would our ability to do anything for God's glory be any different?

Seize the moment and step out in faith today. Maybe there is a neighbor you are supposed to help out today. If only the rich young man had taken steps to obey God, I believe God would have stood in the gap with him. I believe God will stand in the gap for you, too, because your decision to act in faith brings Him glory!

MARK 11
A HOUSE OF PRAYER!

After seven weeks of stay-at-home orders, I am getting a lot of reports of weight gain from people. Separately, but maybe connected, media is reporting a rise in domestic violence. Alcohol sales are way up. People are dealing with the stress, anxiety, and grief of this season in different ways. We are learning a lot about ourselves in this time.

Your mom probably taught you to treat your body like a temple. Surprise! She didn't make that up! The Bible talks about your body being the temple of the Holy Spirit, the dwelling place of God on earth (1 Corinthians 3:16-17; 6:19-20). This is a great truth that we often reference when it comes to what we eat and drink and how we treat our own, and other people's, bodies.

I want to make a connection for you this morning: Jesus proclaims in Mark 11:17, "Is it not written, 'My house shall be called a house of prayer for all the nations'? But you have made it a robbers' den."

Your body can either be a "robbers' den" or a "house of prayer." It all comes down to how you use what God has entrusted to you. How are you dealing with your stress, anxiety, and grief amid your current circumstances? What are you learning about yourself?

Seize the moment and be "a house of prayer for all the nations." This is not only God's best way for you to take care of yourself, but it is also the very design of how He makes Himself known to the nations in and through you. I love how God weaves those two together—what is best for you is also the best way to bring Him glory!

MARK 12
BE FAITHFUL TODAY!

We are all trying to figure out the right next step. What we need right now is a living faith that gives us resiliency! My simple definition of resiliency is this: when you are knocked down, you have the ability not only to get back up, but to bounce forward. The key is having a living and persevering faith.

In Mark 12:11-12, at the end of a parable where Jesus clearly indicates that He knows that He will be betrayed and killed, Jesus quotes from Psalm 118:22-23, "The stone which the builders rejected, this became the chief corner stone; this came about from the LORD, and it is marvelous in our eyes."

The next verse of this Psalm sings, "This is the day which the LORD has made; Let us rejoice and be glad in it" (24).

Jesus told this parable and, while the religious leaders looked for ways to arrest him, Jesus kept on going, not preoccupied with their plans to harm Him, but fully alive in the moment. Jesus had resiliency because He fully trusted His Father with all of His tomorrows.

When you can trust God for tomorrow, you can live faithfully today!

Seize the moment and don't miss today! Be faithful today! Don't miss today's potential for good because you are preoccupied about next week or next month. Call someone and sing: "This is the Day which the LORD has made; Let us rejoice and be glad in it!" Maybe that is all you need to know or do today!

MARK 13
STAY ON GOD'S PLAN!

A story from my college athlete days: It was the 1996 NCAA Division I Track & Field Championships. I was in peak condition, and I was ready to compete at my highest level. But I made a mistake and I paid for it in spades. I let the overwhelming odds of competing against the Hungarian, who would become not only the NCAA Champion that day, but also the gold medalist in the 1996 Olympics a few months later, inside my head. I choked because I veered away from the plan. I allowed my circumstances to take control.

Christians are to remain hopeful in the face of what feels like overwhelming odds. When everything looks out of control, we are to walk by faith and not by sight. We are to stay on God's Plan as His Image Bearers! Reflect on Jesus' reassuring words from Mark 13:23, "But take heed; behold, I have told you everything in advance." and then, in verse 31, "Heaven [the skies] and earth will pass away, but My words will not pass away."

Be assured that, against all evidence presented by media outlets and from our own daily circumstances, the world is not out of control, but rather on a foreseen path towards the completion of all things. God has already told us so that we can remain focused! So that we can stick to the plan!

Seize the moment and remain faithful to God's plan. How are your responses to today's circumstances helping people see God's love and mercy? How are you stirring one another up to love and good works?

MARK 14
PRESS INTO JESUS AND TRUST HIM!

In these stressful days, the elders of our church are pressing into Jesus and trusting Him for wisdom and guidance, safety and protection. How are you handling the stress?

One of the most powerful images of Jesus is found in Mark 14:36, in what could have been one of Jesus' most stressful (and tempting) moments in his earthly ministry. Listen to Jesus pray, "Abba! Father! All things are possible for You; remove this cup from Me; yet not what I will, but what You will."

Under stress, Jesus did two things:

1. He pressed into the intimacy of His relationship with His Father. "Abba" (translated "daddy") was a new way to relate to God; Jesus invites us to see God this way.

2. Jesus pressed into the trust that comes from such an intimate relationship. Trust doesn't come easy for people, but what else does Jesus need to do for you than what He did on the Cross for you to be able to trust Him?

Seize the moment and press into the intimacy of your relationship with God. Trust Him. God loves you, cares about you, and is inviting you right now to trust Him.

MARK 15
TRULY, JESUS IS THE SON OF GOD!

As I write this, the church building has been closed to in-person services for several weeks but is preparing to re-open in the coming days. Our church building's front entrance and portico area are being used as a state COVID-19 testing site for the next several days. Truly, the Church never closed because we are being good partners to bring thriving to our communities. This is why we exist!

Please join us in doing the right thing--BE the Church that Jesus gave His life for!

Listen to Mark 15:39, "When the centurion, who was standing right in front of [Jesus], saw the way He breathed His last, he said, 'Truly this man was the Son of God!'"

Here is a pagan centurion, who watched how Jesus died, declaring, "Truly this man was the Son of God!" My question for you, and us, is this: What do our unbelieving neighbors say about us when they see us using our building for blood drives, financial and practical assistance, food distributions, and COVID-19 testing, even though it is closed to us meeting as a congregation?

Seize the moment and shine the light of Jesus Christ! May your neighbors be able to say the same about Jesus because of the way you live your life: Truly, Jesus is the Son of God!

MARK 16
BELIEF!

What does it mean to believe?

If I say I believe that chair is a good and safe place to sit down and enjoy my morning cup of coffee while I read my Bible, then I act upon it. I put all my weight into it, and I trust the chair to support me. I don't do a half squat in the chair and start feeling the burn within seconds just to keep the illusion that I believe.

Belief is not just an act of the mind to understand a truth, or the will of our hearts to trust. Biblical belief requires the work of God in us to act upon what our minds and hearts say is true. It is the coming together of our whole person into a lifestyle that proclaims what we believe.

The Gospel of Mark concludes with a description of the events of the resurrection, but it doesn't end with an optimistic view of the disciples. Jesus is raised from the dead, but over and over again the disciples struggled to believe. Listen to Mark 16:8, "They went out and fled from the tomb, for trembling and astonishment had gripped them; and they said nothing to anyone, for they were afraid."

Mark continues to say of the disciples, "they refused to believe it" (11) and again, "they did not believe them either" (13). Jesus gave three eyewitnesses a personal encounter, but the disciples would not believe.

Seize the moment and pray that Holy Spirit will work in you to align your lifestyle (from the inside out) to the teachings of Jesus Christ. The evidence of belief is not displayed in what building you find yourself sitting on a Sunday morning (That's truer than ever!) but in how you live for Jesus all week long. Don't get distracted from being the Church—Shine the light of Jesus Christ!

LUKE

LUKE 1
MAY IT BE TO ME AS GOD SAYS!

The Gospel of Luke is the third of the Synoptic Gospels. Big word alert! Synoptic simply means "same view" and when used of the Gospels of Matthew, Mark, and Luke it means that these three authors generally see the ministry of Jesus from the same view, which is quite different from John's Gospel. Some people have made a big deal about these differences and have called it the "synoptic problem," but I assure you there is no substantial problem here.

As we start with Luke 1 today, it is my hope that you have been reading each chapter along with the accompanying devotion. If so, keep it up because you are doing it, maybe for the first time—reading and learning about the Jesus of the Bible for yourself. I invite you to start today if you have not yet been reading along. Fall in love with the Jesus of the Bible.

Consider memorizing Mary's simple words from Luke 1:38, "Behold, the bondslave of the Lord; may it be done to me according to your word." God had just delivered an important message to Mary, and that was her response. God is still in the business of delivering important messages to people and He primarily uses His Word. So, as you go to read your Bible, pray these words, "I am the Lord's servant, may it be to me as God says."

The real problem in contemporary Christianity is not with scholarly issues like the "synoptic problem," but comes when people say they are a Christian, but never spend time with Jesus and, therefore, don't look or sound anything like Him.

Seize the moment and spend time with Jesus, the lover of your soul, today, and He will transform you from the inside out. I am praying for you as you do this.

LUKE 2
I AM ONE OF YOU!

Luke 2:1 begins the classic Christmas story with a worldly power play: "Now in those days a decree went out from Caesar Augustus, that a census be taken of all the inhabited earth."

From the very beginning of the Christmas story is the juxtaposition between God's way of showing His greatness, and how people of the world attempt to show their power.

The world leader, Caesar Augustus, wants everyone to see his greatness so he orders a census of all the people under his control. Caesar, acting as a sovereign over the Roman Empire, disrupts the lives of so many so that he can show himself greater than all under his authority. Essentially, the world's way is to say, "I am better than you, and I'll prove it to you—just watch me!"

God, the true Sovereign, demonstrates His greatness in Luke 2, not by setting Himself apart from His people, but by saying, "I am willing to become one of you!" The incarnation is the visible expression of God's greatness! Jesus meekly left Heaven and came to Earth to show us the way back to the Father (Philippians 2:5-11). Jesus came not to tear us down, but to elevate us (Ephesians 2:6-7) by saying "I am with you!" and, even more radically, "I am one of you!"

While Caesar was busy showing the world how great he was by counting all of his people, God was showing His greatness by becoming one of His people. Immanuel—God is with us!

Seize the moment and follow the way of Jesus Christ. Jesus came to save people and build them up with His words and actions. Jesus came from Heaven to Earth to serve you; how far are you willing to go to help someone else in their needs?

LUKE 3
U-TURNS TO GOD!

As we have worked through these unprecedented times, we have tried to be great partners with our communities to the glory of God by being the Church every day to people in need. Why is this so important? So, we don't have to do a U-turn later!

Speaking of U-turns, did you know that is what the word repentance means? Repentance is a word of freedom and love. In Luke 3:8a, John the Baptizer admonished, "Bear fruits in keeping with repentance."

What a beautiful image! John cautions his audience not to assume they are already connected to God but urges them to enter into a relationship with God. He advises them, and us, to do a U-turn and come home! It will become visible in your words and deeds.

Jesus builds upon this image in John 15:16, "You did not choose Me, but I chose you, and appointed you that you would go and bear fruit, and that your fruit would remain."

Both John and Jesus invite us to repent from assumptions and presumptions that keep us disconnected from God's power and, by repenting, to produce the good fruit that shows it.

Seize the moment and do a U-turn into the arms of God this morning. No matter what your yesterday looked like, God is waiting for you to U-turn back to Him today. His mercies are new every morning. Welcome God into each day and watch what He will do in and through you to His glory.

LUKE 4
AS WAS HIS CUSTOM!

Over my first decade serving at FBC, I have heard many people say that they are lost without gathering for church on Sunday morning. Why? Because it is such an engrained habit that it has become their custom.

Customs are good; Jesus had customs. Listen to Luke 4:16, "And He came to Nazareth, where He had been brought up; and as was His custom, He entered the synagogue on the Sabbath, and stood up to read." We see this in verse 44, "So [Jesus] kept on preaching in the synagogues of Judea." However, we must assess and know what motivates and shapes our customs.

Jesus' customs were motivated and shaped by His mission to proclaim the good news (gospel) of the Kingdom of God. Going to the Jewish meeting place was His custom because that is what God's plan for His life required of Him. For Jesus, His life mission shaped His custom—to seek and to save that which was lost (Luke 19:10), and Jewish synagogues were where His target audience met (Matthew 15:24).

As a pastor-teacher, I have continued to enter the Christian meeting place multiple times every week because my mission shapes my customs, which are to get the word out about Jesus, by whatever means necessary, to empower and equip you, the church, to trust and obey Jesus with your entire life (Ephesians 4:11-16). God's call upon my life shapes and directs my customs. I seek not to draw a crowd, but to mobilize the church into the community!

What shapes and directs your customs?

Seize the moment: "Trust and obey, for there is no other way to be happy in Jesus."

LUKE 5
I AM WILLING!

I spent close to a dozen years on active-duty military service in the US Army. It was an all-volunteer army which means that every single person who was following orders allowed their own lives to be significantly inconvenienced for the sake of the mission. These veterans, my brothers and sisters, were willing to sacrifice their own freedoms to defend the freedoms of those who either could not, or would not, do the same for them. I honor our veterans and I pray for them.

In Luke 5:12-13, a man "covered with leprosy" begged Jesus, "'Lord, if You are willing, You can make me clean.' And [Jesus] stretched out His hand and touched him, saying, 'I am willing; be cleansed.' And immediately the leprosy left him.'"

What a wonderful miracle! What was Jesus' next move? In our experience with religion, a revival tent would have gone up in verse 15 to accommodate the "large crowds" who wanted to hear Jesus and be healed. But that wasn't Jesus' next move! Verse 16 says, "But Jesus Himself would often slip away to the wilderness and pray."

Jesus was on a mission and, while most people hear that kind of language about Jesus' life, they may not realize that this is military language. Jesus was under orders from His Father; so, while the people wanted to take control of His plans and schedules, Jesus broke off to listen to His Father. Rather than following the crowds, Jesus stayed on mission!

You see, being on mission means you have to know your marching orders from God for each and every day.

Seize the moment: Before you let other people take over your life in the name of Christian charity or church volunteerism, spend some time with God to listen to your day's marching orders. Who is directing your steps—your emotions, other people, or God?

LUKE 6
STAY IN YOUR OWN LANE!

When you drive down the street, do you stay inside your lane? If you leave your lane, what could happen?

Jesus commands us in Luke 6:37-38, "Do not judge, and you will not be judged; and do not condemn, and you will not be condemned; pardon, and you will be pardoned. Give, and it will be given to you. They will pour into your lap a good measure—pressed down, shaken together, and running over. For by your standard of measure it will be measured to you in return."

You will be judged by the same measure you use to judge others. The hope in Jesus' words is that you will not judge others, but rather that you will give others the same abundant forgiveness that you yourself received from Him. This command comes with the promises of God for those who are generous as good stewards of all that they have!

You are not called to be a judge of souls (that God's job alone), a prosecutor of people's intentions (only God knows the heart!), or a defense attorney for God. You are called to be an eyewitness of the forgiveness and grace freely given to you.

Stay in your lane and let the Holy Spirit do the work of convicting people of their sin. Let the Word of God do the judging—it is living and active, sharper than a double-edged sword (Hebrews 4:12). We don't need to add our sharp tongues to the Word's effectiveness!

Seize the moment and receive the forgiveness and grace of Jesus Christ in your life, today. If you stay in your lane, there are always great opportunities to tell other people about what God has done for you. Will you be usable to God by staying in the lane He has assigned to you? To whom does God want you to give, or forgive, by His grace today?

LUKE 7
HUMILITY!

Do you believe what people say about you? It's a dangerous business finding yourself on the front page of the newspaper. Why? Because you might believe what the world says about you. Once we start believing opinions, whose opinion matters the most?

In Luke 7:1-10, we read a powerful story of how Jesus heals the servant of a Roman centurion. Verses 3-5 narrate the story as the "Jewish elders … earnestly implored [Jesus], saying, '[the Centurion] is worthy for You to grant this to him; for he loves our nation and it was he who built us our synagogue.'"

I am a bit scandalized by the use of the word "worthy," and of a Jewish endorsement for an occupying force's military leader in their hometown. It strikes me as flattery, but the centurion did not believe his own press release, nor give himself over to flattery (6-7). Unlike his emperor, who demanded that people worship him as a god, here was a humble man. Jesus concludes about the centurion, "I say to you, not even in Israel have I found such great faith" (9).

This was high praise from Jesus, not flattery! Jesus saw the fruit of repentance in this man. Jesus saw humility instead of pride, love of his neighbor rather than love of self, and a sincere desire to serve his community rather than to be served.

Seize the moment and pray with me: "Lord, I desire to be a faithful person from the inside out. I know that I cannot produce the fruit of repentance on my own power, so please teach me to abide in You so that You can bear fruit through my life for Your glory. In Jesus' name, Amen."

LUKE 8
REACH OUT TO JESUS!

Is there a place in your life where you need to experience the power of Jesus Christ?

In today's chapter, there is the story of a woman who has been suffering for twelve years and, at great personal risk, she reaches out to touch Jesus. This poor woman had been ostracized by her community and had been drained of all of her financial resources. She was destitute and desperate because no one could help her with her infirmity—a twelve-year hemorrhage. Not only was this bleeding threatening to take her life, but it had also already robbed her of her quality of life.

Then Jesus came to town, and she knew that her only hope was a miracle from Jesus. What did she do? The only thing she knew to do—she reached out to touch Him.

Luke 8:46 demonstrates that Jesus knew that someone had personally reached out to Him: "But Jesus said, 'Someone did touch Me, for I was aware that power had gone out of Me.'"

Many people were part of this crowd that was pressing against Jesus, but Jesus said power went out from Him to one specific person. This woman had touched Jesus in a different way—with faith!

There is a difference between being a part of a clamoring crowd and being a person who reaches out to Jesus in faith. Have you experienced the power of reaching out to Jesus in faith?

Seize the moment and reach out to touch Jesus. May Jesus' power enter into your life, and the circumstances of your greatest needs, as you reach out to Him in faith today.

LUKE 9
STAY ON COURSE IN LIFE!

How do you handle rejection?

Listen to how Jesus handled rejection in Luke 9:51, "He was determined to go to Jerusalem."

In Luke 9:53-56, we see that the disciples of Jesus responded to rejection by getting upset and wanting to call fire from heaven to destroy those who rejected them. But that is not the way of Jesus! Jesus taught His followers a better way than the normal "knee-jerk response."

Here are three simple (but not always easy) steps you can use to deal with rejection:

1. **Pray**. Acknowledge your feelings, for they are real, but instead of letting them take you over, immediately pray and cast the situation on God alone. You won't hurt Him.

2. **Guard your tongue**. Rejection can lead to a wildfire of emotions inside you. Once that wildfire comes out of you, there is no way of taking it back. Don't light the match with words or actions.

3. **Stay focused on God's path for your life**. The way to Jerusalem was the path of Jesus' obedience. Make a decision to refuse to take offense at people and their opinions. Don't get sucked into a toxic response; God has a better plan for your emotions, thoughts, and energy.

Seize the moment and stay focused on God's path for you and live a life of obedience to Jesus. Remember Jesus' words from Luke 9:23, "If anyone wishes to come after Me, he must deny himself, and take up his cross daily and follow Me."

LUKE 10
SOUL CARE!

You have heard it said, put on your own oxygen mask first. This illustration comes from air travel for people traveling with a child. The point is that if you are impaired, or unconscious, from a lack of oxygen, you can't help someone else.

How do you keep first things first in your life? More pointedly, how is it with your soul?

As a culture of "Marthas," we are an anxious people who want to be busy. It's understandable, but I wonder how many people actually stopped long enough inside their own heads and hearts to learn what Jesus was trying to communicate. In Luke 10:38-42, Jesus responded to Martha's complaint about Mary, who had actually stopped all her busyness to sit at the feet of Jesus and reflect upon His presence and teachings.

Listen to Jesus' answer in verses 41-42, "Martha, Martha, you are worried and bothered about so many things; but only one thing is necessary, for Mary has chosen the good part, which shall not be taken away from her."

Our culture's anxiety is most visible in the way people communicate—to one another and about one another—and in how miserably-happy people seem to be as they live life "worried and bothered about so many things." It's almost as if when we aren't worried and upset about something, then we think something is really wrong. At the heart of it all, our souls are sick because they are weary and heavy-burdened by many things.

Well, my fellow Marthas, what is paying the steepest price of our soul sickness is our relationships—with God and one another! I'm putting on my own oxygen mask, because who of us really wants to live their lives "worried and bothered about so many things?"

Seize the moment and stop to sit at Jesus' feet today. Jesus gives you a choice.

LUKE 11
HUMILITY IN THE INFORMATION AGE!

Did you know that the evidence you are looking for to support your point of view will always be there for you to find? You will be looking first for that information and will filter out all the rest. Plus, it's easier now in the information age to explore and get support for any possible point of view on the Internet. The problem is not a lack of information out there, but it's in how we allow the information to shape our hearts and how we do relationships.

In Luke 11:53-54, the religious leaders had set their hearts against Jesus; they had already made up their minds: "When [Jesus] left there, the scribes and the Pharisees began to be very hostile and to question Him closely on many subjects, plotting against Him to catch Him in something He might say."

The real issue is an ancient one: pride! The answer is found in the character of Jesus, who is gentle and humble in heart (Matthew 11:29). Humility is a learned quality in a person that allows for healthy relationships and brings about thriving communities. Pride destroys both relationships and communities!

The religious leaders of Jesus' day stopped listening to Jesus and were only trying to "catch him" to prove they were right, and he was wrong. I am saddened by how many people today are doing the same as these ancient pharisees. If we can ever have a conversation again, a real dialogue, or a healthy debate on a topic, we must be humble.

As Peter says in 1 Peter 5:5, "All of you, clothe yourselves with humility toward one another, for God is opposed to the proud, but gives grace to the humble."

Seize the moment and pray for God to humble you. This will do a world of good for you, your relationships, and our communities.

LUKE 12
WORRY ROBS THE PRESENT!

Just last night, a dear sister in Christ was sharing with me about her family and updating prayer requests with me when she said, "Now we look forward at the uncertainty of the next school year, making preparations, but trying not to dwell on the "what if's". Living in the present moment is so challenging, even when that is basically the only option available to us right now!"

My advice to them, and any person or family in the same situation is simple, but simple is not always easy: **Don't let your worry about tomorrow rob you of your joy today!**

Jesus taught us in Luke 12:25-26, "And which of you by worrying can add a single hour to his life's span? If then you cannot do even a very little thing, why do you worry about other matters?"

It takes humility to live this way, to trust God with all of your tomorrows and not try to control everything around you.

Seize the moment and give God all your worries. He will give you the grace to live for today!

LUKE 13
THE REST OF GOD!

Jesus returned the religious leaders of His day back to God's original design of honoring the Sabbath day in Luke 13:16: "This woman, a daughter of Abraham as she is, whom Satan has bound for eighteen long years, should she not have been released from this bond on the Sabbath day?"

Jesus' ongoing conflict with the religious leaders was because He would not observe their rules for the Sabbath day. Jesus called these rules "heavy burdens"—a yoke of slavery put on the people. Rather, Jesus declared "Freedom!" in His easy yoke of grace where the burden is light.

One of the ways you know you are in the easy yoke of Jesus is your ability to rest—mentally, emotionally, and relationally, not just physically. Are you struggling to rest? Whose yoke are you in?

Your ability to rest mentally and physically from your unfinished work demonstrates your faith in the finished work of Jesus Christ.

Your ability to rest emotionally from your worries and anxieties demonstrates your hope in the sovereign grace of God.

Your ability to rest relationally from your need to have other people meet your needs demonstrates your trust in the Holy Spirit's constant companionship.

We were designed to find our rest in the Trinitarian fellowship of God!

Seize the moment and rest! Can you prioritize time to find the rest of God by not multitasking God with the many other things spinning in your mind, churning in your heart, or on your to-do or honey-do list? I pray that you strive to enter into the rest of God!

LUKE 14
THE HEART OF GOD'S REST!

Luke 14 starts with Jesus in the home of a prominent Pharisee, surrounded by experts in the Law, but there is also a man there who is suffering from dropsy. While it was against the religious rules of the day to do any work on the Sabbath, Jesus asks a question in Luke 14:3 that strikes to the heart of why He came: "Is it lawful to heal on the Sabbath, or not?" As they stare at Jesus blankly, He takes hold of the man and heals him and then asks the experts in Luke 14:5, "Which one of you will have a son or an ox fall into a well, and will you not immediately pull him out on a Sabbath day?"

Jesus came on a rescue mission to pull people out of the effects of the Fall, to bring people Home to His Father, to usher in the rule of God. Jesus was not rebelling against the Sabbath itself; He was actively reforming the Sabbath back to God's original intent. He was demonstrating the Kingdom of God, where it is done on Earth as it is in Heaven. The heart of God's rest is the proclamation of God's rescue from slavery!

When you rest in God you are free from the tyranny of the urgent and you are doing the most important thing! When you rest in God you are pointing back to the seventh day when God ceased from His work to give creation His delight. When you rest in God you are pointing towards the Day of the fullness of God's perfect rule once again: to the New Heaven and New Earth as described in Revelation 21 and 22.

Seize the moment and prioritize time to enter into the rest of God! Will you go and put it on your calendar right now?

LUKE 15
A DAY TO BE THANKFUL!

Who are you thankful for today?

Listen to Luke 15:31-32, "Son, you have always been with me, and all that is mine is yours. But we had to celebrate and rejoice, for this brother of yours was dead and has begun to live, and was lost and has been found."

This is from the Parable of the Lost Son. It emphasizes the two earlier parables "The Lost Sheep" and "The Lost Coin," but this one has a twist in it.

God is the central character of each parable: God is like the good shepherd who goes to great lengths to find the one lost sheep; God is like the woman who goes to great effort to find the one lost coin; and God is like the father who eagerly waited to receive back His lost son.

The twist in this parable is that, unlike the other two, no one went looking for that which was lost. The Father stayed home—Who was supposed to go looking for the younger son?

Luke 15 sets us up with expectancy: Someone is going to go searching for that which was lost; when the older brother doesn't do his job, we are left confused and hurt!

Jesus' parable causes our hearts to yearn for our true elder brother to come search for us: to seek and to save that which was lost.

The three parables not only show us the heart of God but teach us the mission of Jesus Christ. Jesus is the elder Son, sent by His Father, to search for us to bring us Home.

Seize the moment and rejoice in God's rescue of His children! Today is a great day to be thankful! Freedom is not free—the elder Son paid the price! May your life tell His story!

LUKE 16
EVERY SOUL MATTERS!

Each and every person has a soul! Souls are eternal, and each has intrinsic value. That means people matter, regardless of whether you like them, agree with them, or feel like they bring value to you or your view of the world. To relate kindly only to the people who help make your life work better for you may be simply utilitarian to you, but it is evil as a habitual practice. It's dishonest!

The Parable of the Shrewd Steward from Luke 16:1-13, highlights how followers of Jesus are to be household managers of their wealth to influence people for God's glory. Verses 8-9 make the point of the story,

> And his master praised the unrighteous manager because he had acted shrewdly; for the sons of this age are more shrewd in relation to their own kind than the sons of light. And I say to you, make friends for yourselves by means of the wealth of unrighteousness, so that when it fails, they will receive you into the eternal dwellings.

Has God blessed you with the ability to work hard? Praise God! Now win souls by working hard, starting businesses, and creating jobs that produce wealth for the work force, so that more money can go to bless others, support ministries, and fuel the work of the Kingdom.

Has God blessed you with wealth and the influence it brings in the world? Praise God! Our culture values people with money more than all others so use that temporary influence to win souls, because you can lose it all in a heartbeat.

No person is better than another because they have money. So, invest what God has entrusted to you, not into a false sense of self-worth as defined by the world, but into what matters for eternity. Use "stuff" to gain people for God's Kingdom! The harvest fields are ripe. I'm praying for workers!

Seize the moment and make an eternal investment today.

LUKE 17
THE HOME OF GOD!

The concept of being part of a kingdom is so foreign to American sensibilities. We are an independent people; it's a big part of our national identity and self-narrative, so we struggle to understand authority, headship, submission, and all the realities of living under the rule of a king. Therefore, we struggle to know exactly what Jesus is saying when He declares the Kingdom of God.

There is a biblical theme that allows us to understand the kingdom teaching by looking at the Kingdom of God as the Home of God, with God as the Father and with us being restored to His sovereign rule through the headship of Jesus Christ.

Listen to Jesus explain the coming of the Kingdom of God to the Pharisees in Luke 17:20-21: "The kingdom of God is not coming with signs to be observed; nor will they say, 'Look, here it is!' or, 'There it is!' For behold, the kingdom of God is in your midst."

What a beautiful thought: the Home of God is in you! Jesus came to usher us into His Father's Household.

This is your salvation! When you believe in God and put your faith in His Son Jesus Christ, then He seals you with a guarantee through the living presence of the third person of the Trinity—the Holy Spirit (Ephesians 1:14; 2 Corinthians 1:22). Salvation is your invitation to, and participation in, the Trinitarian fellowship of God.

God has made His home in you!

Seize the moment and believe, for the Home of God is here. The Kingdom of God is here, not as a geopolitical empire with borders and laws, but as a home to experience the Father's love for eternity. You are home in God because Jesus made a way for you and the Holy Spirit has made His home in you—rest in God!

LUKE 18
YOUR DEEPEST NEED!

In Luke 18:41, Jesus asks the question, "What do you want Me to do for you?"

The story is told in Luke 18:35-43; a blind beggar cries out: "Jesus, Son of David, have mercy on me!" (38). Even though he is rebuked by those around him, this blind beggar cries out louder and louder: "Son of David, have mercy on me!" (39).

This got Jesus' attention. The blind beggar was socially ridiculed for crying out to Jesus, but he boldly risked their scorn for a chance to get to Jesus. He needed something only God could give him (Luke 18:27). Jesus responded to his faith!

I wonder if you need something that is so deep, so pressing in your life, that you would be willing to face people's rebuke and ridicule to cry out to Jesus. Do you know your deepest need? What would you ask for if you were in the place of this blind beggar?

Not a want...

Not a temporary fix...

Not a Band-Aid on a gushing artery wound...

The truth is, without God in our lives, we are all blind beggars, in need of healing, in need of deliverance, in need of what only He can give. If that truth offends you, maybe that's your deepest need!

Remember these words from Luke 18:27, "The things that are impossible with people are possible with God."

Seize the moment and put yourself in the shoes of this blind beggar from two thousand years ago: If Jesus asked you, "What do you want Me to do for you?" what would you say? I pray for you that the Lord Jesus Christ may lead you into a sincere faith as you cry out to Him today for the deepest need of your life. May the Lord heal, bless, deliver, and rescue you today.

LUKE 19
PRAY FOR OUR NATION!

Listen to Jesus cry out for Jerusalem in Luke 19:41-44,

When He approached Jerusalem, He saw the city and wept over it, saying, "If you had known in this day, even you, the things which make for peace! But now they have been hidden from your eyes. For the days will come upon you when your enemies will throw up a barricade against you, and surround you and hem you in on every side, and they will level you to the ground and your children within you, and they will not leave in you one stone upon another, because you did not recognize the time of your visitation."

Whatever the future may hold, you can trust that the Lord is good and just in all that He does. The Lord is holy and sovereign; whatever may happen, God will use it for His glory. God uses nation-states and empires according to His will and desire. He is the Living Hope for all creation.

Are you putting your hope in Jesus as you watch the news? Are you trusting in Jesus as you see how people are reacting and behaving around our communities?

I invite you to start praying the way Jesus taught His disciples to pray: "Your will be done, on earth as it is in Heaven" (Matthew 6:10b), and then follow Jesus wherever He may lead you. The Church of Jesus Christ is the hope of the nations because we are the hands and feet of Christ to our communities and nations.

Seize the moment and cry out to God for His mercy for our communities and nations. Jesus is the only One who can give us peace. Remain calm and pray—God is with us! There is a perfect storm brewing out there; will you join me in praying today for our nation?

LUKE 20
HONEST CONVERSATIONS!

Do you find it difficult to have an honest conversation with people in today's world?

Luke 20 narrates a series of conversations where the religious leaders are trying to trap Jesus in His words so that they can justify their desire to murder Him. Listen to one in Luke 20:3-7:

> Jesus answered and said to them, "I will also ask you a question, and you tell Me: 'Was the baptism of John from heaven or from men?'" They reasoned among themselves, saying, "If we say, 'From heaven,' He will say, 'Why did you not believe him?' But if we say, 'From men,' all the people will stone us to death, for they are convinced that John was a prophet." So, they answered that they did not know where it came from.

Jesus is trying to expose the duplicity of the religious leaders. They immediately calculate the cost of each answer as if the truth was a commodity to be nuanced and peddled for their power and profit. The religious leaders were not interested in the truth—only themselves.

Are people any better today?

I don't know about you, but I'm tired of what our inability to have an honest conversation is doing to our communities. The truth should not be shaped for influence and power. The truth should not be peddled for personal profit. Jesus said, "the truth will make you free" (John 8:32).

Honest conversations are the only way to have substantial and life-giving relationships.

Is your communication going to be full of double-dealing and calculation, or are you just going to be honest with yourself and others? Do you have a friend in your life you are willing to listen to who will give you honest insights about you and your life?

Seize the moment and start with an honest conversation with God. He's waiting for you.

LUKE 21
KEEP YOUR CHIN UP!

I say to you this morning: Friend of God, don't give yourself over to despair or discouragement. Keep your chin up! It's a choice!

In Luke 21, Jesus foretells the dark days that would usher in His second coming. Jesus says in Luke 21:27-28, "Then they will see the Son of Man coming in a cloud with power and great glory. But when these things begin to take place, straighten up and lift up your heads, because your redemption is drawing near."

I love those words: "straighten up and lift up your heads." In other words, keep your chin up! In the midst of hardship, death, destruction, and so much going the wrong direction in the world, we, the followers of Jesus Christ, are to remain firm in our faith, resolved in our hope, and steadfast in our love.

Why? "Because [our] redemption is drawing near" (28).

Jesus is our Living Redeemer and, as His second-coming draws near, we are to remain watchful and hopeful for Him, allowing our faith to superintend our emotions. No matter what may be happening right now, remember this truth, "My Redeemer lives" (Job 19:25)!

Is there a difficult circumstance you must deal with today? Ask Jesus to walk with you through this time. God is with you—so keep your chin up!

Are you facing a difficult relationship decision? Trust God in your most important decisions and remember that God will never leave you nor forsake you—so keep your chin up!

Seize the moment and make a choice today: Live your life with faith, hope, and love! By keeping your eyes on Jesus, He will keep your chin up!

LUKE 22
VICTORY OVER EVIL!

Do you ever feel like there is an active force opposing you and any good that you try to do?

Years ago, I memorized Jesus' words from Luke 22:31-32, "Simon, Simon, behold, Satan has demanded permission to sift you like wheat; but I have prayed for you, that your faith may not fail; and you, when once you have turned again, strengthen your brothers."

Sifting wheat is a violent action of separating the grain from the stalk and chaff; it is a process of literally tearing the wheat apart. Satan's desire for Simon (called Peter) is to violently tear him apart, to separate him from God's promises and purposes, and to tear Peter away from God's plan for his life. That's what Satan wants to do to all people who confess Jesus as the Son of the living God—"the thief comes only to steal and kill and destroy" (John 10:10)!

Jesus is our Living Redeemer who sits at the right hand of God, the Father, praying for us today. It is by faith that we overcome evil! As the Bible teaches us, "Greater is He who is in us than he who is in the world" (1 John 4:4). If God is for you, who can stand against you?

What can you do when you feel there are forces actively working against you and those you love?

Seize the moment and take the higher ground by praying! Stand firm against Satan, who asks to sift you as wheat. Jesus' promise that your faith will not fail will come true in your life, as it did in Peter's, and as it has in my own life. Turn back to God today and strengthen your family in Christ. Never forget, Jesus is praying for you!

LUKE 23
PREVAILING VOICES!

What voices are winning the day in your life? The loudest? The most emotional? The most pleasing?

These are the questions that come to my mind when I read Luke 23:18-25.

In verse 23, "But they [the crowd of accusers] were insistent, with loud voices asking that [Jesus] be crucified. And their voices began to prevail."

There was no evidence of any guilt. Both Herod and Pilate found no reason to crucify Jesus. But Jesus was sentenced to death anyway!

Then, in verse 24, "And Pilate pronounced sentence that their demand be granted." Pilate released a guilty man (Barabbas) and sentenced an innocent man to death (25).

Why? Because it was politically expedient.

The wrong voices prevailed in his life! The voices of the crowd got louder and more demanding for their own way, even though there was no content or clarity in the words. Have you ever noticed that when people have no strong rationale for their points of view, they often resort to emotionalism, volume, violence, intimidation, or manipulation to get their way?

What voices are prevailing in your life? What voices are prevailing in your home and in your church? What voices are prevailing in our communities and our country?

The Spirit of Truth invites you today to get quiet so that you can listen to the wisdom of God's Word through the Bible and prayer. The Holy Spirit wants to teach you through your Bible reading, that you may hide His word in your heart so that you can apply it in your daily life.

Seize the moment and pay attention to what voices you are allowing to prevail in you. If it is not God's Word guiding you, who or what is really prevailing in your life? Your life will reflect the god you serve.

LUKE 24
HEART ON FIRE!

What causes your heart to burn within you? Is it heartburn or is there a passion inside your heart?

There's a big difference!

In Luke 24:13-35, the story of Jesus revealing Himself to two of His disciples occurs over the sharing of a meal. Jesus had walked from Jerusalem to Emmaus with them and they did not know that they were walking with the resurrected Lord, but, in the sharing of a meal, their eyes were opened as Jesus breaks the bread. Reflect on verses 30-32,

> When He had reclined at the table with them, He took the bread and blessed it, and breaking it, He began giving it to them. Then their eyes were opened, and they recognized Him; and He vanished from their sight. They said to one another, "Were not our hearts burning within us while He was speaking to us on the road, while He was explaining the Scriptures to us?"

Did the bread Jesus served them give them heartburn? No, the phrase is an idiom! The resurrected Jesus excited them—they felt passion as He opened up the Word to them as He walked and talked with them. His presence lit a fire in their hearts!

Seize the moment and go to the table to meet with Jesus each and every day. The resurrected Lord wants to meet with you and break bread with you. Don't let the stress of your circumstances give you heartburn but let Jesus' presence with you set your heart on fire!

JOHN

JOHN 1
GOD'S EMPATHY TO BECOME ONE OF US!

Recent events have highlighted an empathy OPPORTUNITY in our country, communities, and churches! For too long, we have been such an egocentric people that we can't imagine that someone else might see a situation different than us. If we are going to have a future, we must learn empathy! This is the ability to share the feelings and experiences of another person—to put on their skin and to walk in their shoes. With empathy, a lot of wonderful conversations would begin. This is our time and Christians are the ones who can change everything!

Why us?

Because Christianity was birthed in empathy! Our whole faith is about the empathy of a holy God for His lost children. Listen to John 1:14, "And the Word became flesh and dwelt among us, and we saw His glory, glory as of the only begotten from the Father, full of grace and truth."

This is one of my favorite verses about Jesus' birth. God, who is spirit, took on flesh and dwelt among us; this is the Incarnation! Jesus Christ is God's empathy—He literally put on our skin and walked in our sandals.

Why would God, who is holy and sovereign over all things, do such a thing? Why did God enter into our human experience and become one of us?

Love! That's why! God shared in a human's temporary life so that we can forever live in God's eternal life! Empathy is driven by love and for love! Empathy is the way of Jesus!

Seize the moment and learn to walk in the sandals of Jesus. In doing so, He will lead you to be willing to show empathy.

JOHN 2
LIVING FOR AN AUDIENCE OF ONE!

Who determines whether you are doing a good job in your life? Whose opinion of you is shaping your personal well-being and the efforts of your life?

In John 2:23-25, Jesus responded to the clamoring of people,

Now when He was in Jerusalem at the Passover, during the feast, many believed in His name, observing His signs which He was doing. But Jesus, on His part, was not entrusting Himself to them, for He knew all men, and because He did not need anyone to testify concerning him, for He Himself knew what was in man.

So quickly, Jesus' actions have caused both great applause and passionate anger. With these came the very human pressure to give Himself over to their attention and opinions. Jesus did not!

Jesus was focused on leading people out of slavery to their own sin, and Jesus couldn't set us free if He was enslaved to our fickle public opinion polls. Jesus did not allow either the complaints, or the applause, to get into His heart or mind. He stayed true to His Father's words and secure in His Father's love.

Our culture teaches us the value of self-worth, but even that, when we are honest, is slavery of the highest order—to self! Jesus came to give each of us a Christ-worth that is given in love, established by faith, and sealed for eternity by God's Holy Spirit making His home in us!

May our views of ourselves be determined by how much Jesus loves us. It is only in Jesus' love that we are set free to truly love others because we are now secure in the Father's love.

Seize the moment and be free of the public opinion polls in your own life. Give 100% of your heart loyalty to Jesus and live for an audience of One and the applause of His nail-scarred hands!

JOHN 3
MAKE MORE OF HIM!

When people are going through a prolonged season of hardship, one of my recommendations to them is to find ways to love and serve other people. Why? Because it's good medicine for their souls! It takes their attention off of themselves and refocuses it on helping another person.

Listen to a portion of John the Baptizer's famous statement about himself in John 3:27-30,

A man can receive nothing unless it has been given him from heaven. You yourselves are my witnesses that I said, "I am not the Christ," but, "I have been sent ahead of Him." He who has the bride is the bridegroom; but the friend of the bridegroom, who stands and hears him, rejoices greatly because of the bridegroom's voice. So this joy of mine has been made full. He must increase, but I must decrease.

As Christians, we are the bride of Christ—with Jesus as our bridegroom! You are a friend of God! What great joy it brings into your life to tell others about Jesus! May you experience the fullness of joy as you share the love of God with people, in word and deed.

This is how we make more of Him and less of ourselves. Not by tearing ourselves down, or having a false humility, but by living our lives for His glory. John has given us the recipe for a joy-filled life. Be a friend of God, be the bride of Christ, and make more of Him than you do of yourself!

Seize the moment because you have an opportunity today to increase the name of Jesus in your own life, in the lives of your family and friends, and in the lives of coworkers and classmates. Pray right now to have your heart and mind open to each opportunity.

JOHN 4
FINDING COMMON GROUND WITH PEOPLE!

Have you ever ended up having a meaningful conversation with someone you didn't know very well? Have you ever initiated a spiritual conversation that was difficult for you?

John 4 shares with us the story of Jesus' unplanned conversation with a Samaritan woman who went midday to get her water from the well. The timing of her getting water, when the other women were not there, indicates she was a social outcast. But by the end of the story, this one conversation with Jesus transformed her life and she became the catalyst of change for her community. This all came about because of what appears to be a circumstantial conversation that leads from a request for water to the offer of eternal life.

Jesus started the conversation on common ground with a safe request in John 4:7, "Give Me a drink." While we see amazing, miraculous events unfold from this encounter, I just want us to dwell on this moment. For many of us, the biggest miracle would be to reach out to someone we don't know to initiate a spiritual conversation with them.

It will change your life if you start training yourself to look for common ground with people instead of focusing on what is different about you and another person. Remember, you will always find what you are looking for. If you are looking for a bridge between you and another person, you will find it. If you are looking for a barrier, you will also find that.

Seize the moment and build bridges with people by looking for common ground with them. Ask God to give you open eyes, and a willing heart, to follow Jesus into a conversation. You never know how one spiritual conversation can transform a person's life.

JOHN 5
ABSOLUTE DEPENDENCE ON JESUS!

It's not a common image anymore, but it was a common sight, from the times of Jesus up to not very long ago, even here in rural Indiana. Two animals were often seen united by a yoke in order to share the burden of the work by going two-by-two into the fields. This agricultural image is one of my favorite concepts of following Jesus—not just for ministry work, but for everyday life.

Listen to Jesus discuss His life and ministry in the yoke of His Father. From John 5:19-20,

> Truly, truly, I say to you, the Son can do nothing of Himself; unless it is something that He sees the Father doing; for whatever the Father does, these things the Son also does in like manner. For the Father loves the Son, and shows Him all things that He Himself is doing; and the Father will show Him greater works than these, so that you will marvel.

Jesus is giving glory to the Father after He heals a great many people. But what did Jesus do? He pointed people to the source and inspiration of all of His works—His relationship with the Father!

God's heart for each of us is to be yoked with Christ so that His word can direct our steps, and the Holy Spirit can bear fruit in our lives, all for the glory of the Father! All that we can think to do, or have the power to do, flows out of our intimate union with Christ. Apart from Him, we can do nothing. It was the same for Jesus!

Seize the moment and submit your day to Jesus by getting in His yoke every morning through prayer, scripture reading, and times of invitation to His presence. Don't go into the fields by yourself. It is only in absolute dependence on God that we can do the works that God has for us to do.

JOHN 6
FRESH BREAD!

Do you enjoy fresh bread, whether homemade or store bought? Do you have a favorite doughnut shop, where you can get a fresh doughnut? I think we all would agree that fresh bread is better than stale bread, or even day-old bread.

John 6 is so rich, so packed full of the life-giving teachings of Jesus. Listen to Jesus serve fresh bread in verses 35-40,

> I am the bread of life; he who comes to Me will not hunger, and he who believes in Me will never thirst. But I said to you that you have seen Me, and yet do not believe. All that the Father gives Me will come to Me, and the one who comes to Me I will certainly not cast out. For I have come down from heaven, not to do My own will, but the will of Him who sent Me. This is the will of Him who sent Me, that of all that He has given Me I lose nothing, but raise it up on the last day. For this is the will of My Father, that everyone who beholds the Son and believes in Him will have eternal life, and I Myself will raise him up on the last day.

Seize the moment and enjoy the fresh bread of Jesus' words. Hear Jesus' daily invitation to sit and enjoy His presence in your quiet time with Him—Come to Me, all who are hungry and thirsty, and I will satisfy your heart, mind, body, and soul. Jesus wants to give you fresh bread today.

JOHN 7
DISCOURAGEMENT DERAILS!

Do you ever feel discouraged and just want to quit?

In John 7:5, we learn this about Jesus' ministry, "For not even His brothers were believing in Him." In verse 1 we learn that Jesus stayed away from Judea because the Jewish authorities "were seeking to kill Him."

Have you ever felt like you could do better if you had people in your corner who believed in you? If you only had more support, and less opposition?

Jesus knew what it was like to have an unsupportive family, but He did not let that discourage Him from being faithful to do God's will in His life. In fact, from a human perspective, Jesus had much more going against Him, because not only was His family not believing in Him, but the religious systems were actively against Him, and the support system He did have was composed of a ragamuffin group of followers that didn't seem to get it half of the time.

Many people would have just quit and moved on! Working in a situation with a lack of support, with active opposition, and with constant misunderstanding is a breeding ground for discouragement. But Jesus kept His eyes on the Father—on God's love for Him and on God's will for His life. That kept Jesus securely centered on who He was and why He was doing what He was doing. Jesus listened to the right voice!

Do you let discouragement derail you? Do you allow setbacks to prevent you from going forward? Do you focus on the ones who do not believe in you, or the One who does believe in you?

Seize the moment and keep your eyes on Jesus, the author and finisher of your faith. When you are feeling discouraged and want to quit, get back in the yoke of Jesus and trust God to help you finish strong.

JOHN 8
FREEDOM!

Kimberly and I traveled to Scotland for our 20th wedding anniversary, and as I walked in the Highlands I cried out at the top of my lungs, FREEDOM! Just like William Wallace in the movie Braveheart! This great man from Scottish history gave His life at 35 for Scotland to be free from English tyrannical rule.

Jesus Christ gave His life for all of humanity to be free by rescuing us from Satan's grasp and sin's oppression!

Are you free?

Jesus exclaims in John 8:36, "So if the Son makes you free, you will be free indeed."

You are free to be generous and giving.
You are free to be loving and forgiving.
You are free to be caring and serving.

You are free to reflect the glory of God by how you love, care, and steward God's creation! He designed you and made you to be an Image Bearer!

Jesus submitted His own life, words, and actions to the will of His Father. He gave up His rights and emptied Himself (Philippians 2:5-11), not to live for Himself, but to give His life as a ransom for many (Matthew 20:28). We marvel at Jesus, at His life and His death—at His freedom in both!

You are free to live in the Spirit for Jesus—to be alive in Christ. I pray for you, that you will live the truth of Galatians 5:1: "It was for freedom that Christ set us free; therefore keep standing firm and do not be subject again to a yoke of slavery."

Seize the moment: Be generous—give today to display your freedom from fear. Be loving—forgiving today to demonstrate deliverance from hate. Be caring—serve others today to declare your rescue from self.

JOHN 9
DON'T BAIL BEFORE THE BLESSING!

Here is some common counsel I give people: "Don't bail before the blessing!"

So often, we miss out on God's best for our lives because we don't persevere and we grow weary in doing good. So often, we miss out on God's best for our relationships because we grow callouses around our hearts and get bitter, then we stop giving and forgiving.

Love never fails! Don't bail before the blessing!

I believe God makes use of us in every situation to bring about His greater purposes for His glory. No matter what you are going through, ask yourself, "How can I bring God glory in and through my attitudes, actions, and responses?"

Our lives and our relationships are always about something more than we know.

No matter how overwhelming your situation, remember that there is something greater than you can see at stake. In John 9, when Jesus' disciples asked why a certain man was born blind and whose sin caused it, Jesus responded with a bigger story in mind. Listen to Jesus in John 9:3, "It was neither that this man sinned, nor his parents; but it was so that the works of God might be displayed in him."

Jesus wants to tell the bigger story of God's creation and redemption through your life. It's not just a "once upon a time" story, but an everyday-in-every-way story. A key ingredient to this happening in you is faith—the ability to see and believe in the bigger story of God.

Remember, what is impossible for us, is not impossible for God!

Do you believe God can use your story to tell His Story? Do you have the faith that allows your every-day-every-way story to put God's glory on display?

Seize the moment and don't bail before the blessing! Live by faith and not by sight! God's got this—Trust Him!

JOHN 10
JESUS IS THE SHEPHERD OF MY SOUL!

Kimberly and I have three children, ages thirteen, nine, and six. We are very selective with who watches them. We care deeply about who influences them and who we share authority with in raising them. Raising children is about shepherding their hearts like Jesus shepherds our souls. We work hard to give them a safe home to experience fullness of life.

We need to be just as intentional and selective, if not more, about our own lives: Who do we allow to shepherd our hearts? Who do we invite into the most influential places of our hearts, minds, bodies, and souls to love and nurture us?

John 10 is a beautiful chapter, as Jesus declares that He is the Good Shepherd. Listen to some of Jesus' powerful promises and beautiful teachings from John 10:27-30,

> My sheep hear My voice, and I know them, and they follow Me; and I give eternal life to them, and they will never perish; and no one will snatch them out of My hand. My Father, who has given them to Me, is greater than all, and no one is able to snatch them out of the Father's hand. I and the Father are one.

God loves you! He knows you by name and He cares about you; He wants to be the Good Shepherd of your soul! A Good Shepherd will not only lead you, but He will also protect you and keep you secure in His embrace while tending to your needs.

We are all like sheep who need a good shepherd to bring us into the safety of a good home so that we, too, can experience the John 10:10 promise of the fullness of life.

Seize the moment and ask Jesus Christ to be the Good Shepherd of your soul. He is calling for you—Can you hear His voice?

JOHN 11
UNBINDING LAZARUS!

Do you have anything in your life that is binding you—holding you back—from being the best version of you?

In John 11:44, we read the last words of Jesus in the famous story of how Jesus raised Lazarus from the dead: "The man who had died came forth, bound hand and foot with wrappings, and his face was wrapped around with a cloth. Jesus said to them, 'Unbind him, and let him go.'"

It is so easy to romanticize this story that we forget the very real details and implications. Lazarus was raised from the dead by Jesus, but it took the community to practically, hands-on unbind him from his burial wrap, the linen strips wrapped around his body.

Jesus commanded them to unbind him because it wasn't effective to do it alone!

Here is a practical application: If we are going to participate with God in helping transform stories through the gospel of Jesus Christ then we need to trust Him to do what we can't—resurrect the dead. However, we still have to do what we can: allow people to unbind us from our burial wrap.

Is there anything binding you? Do you need help getting unbound from some stinking thinking or habitual sin patterns that are still affecting your present and infecting your future?

Seize the moment: Let's be a community like the one that came around Lazarus. We unbind one another by forgiving each other often, because we make a mess of things, and helping one another learn how to live as new creations in Jesus. We call this discipleship—we call this doing life together! We all need this in every season of our lives.

JOHN 12
MY SOUL IS TROUBLED!

Is your soul troubled from all that is happening in our nation and communities?

There were times when Jesus' soul was troubled, too; listen to John 12:23-33:

> And Jesus answered them, saying, "The hour has come for the Son of Man to be glorified. Truly, truly, I say to you, unless a grain of wheat falls into the earth and dies, it remains alone; but if it dies, it bears much fruit. He who loves his life loses it, and he who hates his life in this world will keep it to life eternal. If anyone serves Me, he must follow Me; and where I am, there My servant will be also; if anyone serves Me, the Father will honor him. Now My soul has become troubled; and what shall I say, 'Father, save Me from this hour'? But for this purpose I came to this hour. Father, glorify Your name.'" Then a voice came out of heaven: "I have both glorified it, and will glorify it again." Jesus answered and said, "This voice has not come for My sake, but for your sakes. Now judgment is upon this world; now the ruler of this world will be cast out. And I, if I am lifted up from the earth, will draw all men to Myself." But He was saying this to indicate the kind of death by which He was to die.

Seize the moment and answer the call to follow Jesus. He knew the suffering that would come and the hardship that His followers would face in this life. Jesus set us an example to follow, with His life and death. When you feel that you are looking death in the face, please know that God is with you and has already won the victory.

JOHN 13
THE TOWEL OF SERVICE!

Will you put on the "towel of service" for those you love?

Listen to John 13:4-5, "[Jesus] laid aside His garments; and taking a towel, He girded Himself. Then He poured water into the basin and began to wash the disciples' feet and to wipe them with the towel with which He was girded."

Jesus then taught in verses 13-15, "You call me Teacher and Lord, and you are right, for so I am. If I then, your Lord and Teacher, have washed your feet, you also ought to wash one another's feet. For I have given you an example, that you also should do just as I have done to you."

I have heard many people say that they are willing to die for their loved ones. Such bravado! Peter essentially said the same about Jesus in John 13:37, "Lord, why can I not follow You right now? I will lay down my life for You." In the same way that Peter failed to live up to his bravado, so do most people. Because as long as we keep on our outer garments, we will always talk a good game of following Jesus, but will never become like Him.

Why is it we say we are willing to sacrifice everything for the people we love, when we can't even suspend our own self-interests long enough to serve them? What is keeping us from being fully present to the people we love? What are the outer "garments" we must put aside to put on the towel of service?

Seize the moment and be like Jesus. Take off the outer "garments" of how you want to see yourself, and how you want everyone to know you, and put on the towel of service. It is only in the posture of humility that you can become like Jesus and fulfill God's will for your life.

JOHN 14
YOUR HEART, YOUR CHOICE!

I was out trail running recently when my left foot kicked a small root and tripped me up. Down I went—and I mean down hard! Have you ever fallen? Been tripped up? Gone down hard?

Jesus says in John 14:1, "Do not let your heart be troubled; believe in God, believe also in Me" and again later emphasizes in verse 27, "Peace I leave with you; My peace I give to you; not as the world gives do I give to you. Do not let your heart be troubled, nor let it be fearful."

Do you hear your choice? "Do not let your heart be troubled" are the bookends of Jesus' teaching. Jesus calls us to something greater than our flesh response to our circumstances; He calls us to faith in the Prince of Peace! He calls us to make a choice about our hearts!

Be thou at peace, beloved of God! Jesus invites us to rest in Him. One of the great reasons we can rest in God is because Jesus' teaching calls us to the new life of the Holy Spirit! Jesus teaches us that we have a constant companion who is our Helper!

When you are tripped up and you go down hard, what will you do? Will you roll around in the dirt cursing yourself and the world, or will you get back up, brush yourself off, and keep running the race? Life is hard! No one ever promised anything different than that. But, with faith, your witness can show the glory of God!

Seize the moment and get back up! It is natural when you trip for your eyes to head for the ground as you prepare for impact, but the Spirit of God helps you get back up with your eyes on Jesus.

JOHN 15
VINE TIME!

How is your "vine time"?

That's actually a really important question that will make sense to you after you read John 15:1-17. John 15:4-5 starts with Jesus saying to His followers, "Abide in Me, and I in you." Before we read further, allow me to define "abide." It means to remain; to connect with continually. It is an agricultural metaphor that Jesus is using to talk about relationship with Himself—those who answer the call to "follow Me" will abide in Jesus, and He in them.

Let's keep going with Jesus' words, "As the branch cannot bear fruit of itself unless it abides in the vine, so neither can you unless you abide in Me. I am the vine; you are the branches; he who abides in Me and I in him, he bears much fruit, for apart from Me you can do nothing."

We live in a world that asks the question, "What have you produced today? What have you done for me lately?" We live in a culture of ever-increasing transient jobs and utilitarian relationships as people seek first their ambition and desired affluent lifestyle. Loyalty is eroding and, with the decay of that character quality, so are abiding, persevering relationships, even with God.

But that is not the way it is in the Kingdom of God. The Kingdom of God is a relational kingdom and loyalty to Jesus Christ (abiding in the vine) is of the utmost concern. In fact, it is your highest and noblest pursuit, even higher than bearing fruit. Good fruit can only come about from a healthy connection to a good Vine.

How is your connection to Jesus? Is it your priority?

Seize the moment and invest in your Vine time.

JOHN 16
THE HOLY SPIRIT!

Have you ever been confused by of all the different teachings about the Holy Spirit?

Let's keep it simple and read what Jesus says about Him in John 16. Here are a couple snapshots to get you started:

Jesus teaches in verses 7-8, "But I tell you the truth, it is to your advantage that I go away; for if I do not go away, the Helper will not come to you; but if I go, I will send Him to you. And He, when He comes, will convict the world concerning sin and righteousness and judgment."

He continues in verses 13-14, "But when He, the Spirit of truth, comes, He will guide you into all the truth; for He will not speak on His own initiative, but whatever He hears, He will speak; and He will disclose to you what is to come. He will glorify Me, for He will take of Mine and will disclose it to you."

This is my prayer for you as you continue to learn to walk in the Spirit: May the Holy Spirit convict you of sin, righteousness, and judgment so that you may live a holy life to exalt the name of Jesus, to the glory of the Father. May the Holy Spirit teach you and remind you of all that Jesus taught so that your life may bring glory to the name of Jesus, by which a person can be saved. May the Holy Spirit bring glory to Jesus in your life, through the visible evidence of the Fruit of the Spirit in your character (Galatians 5:22-23) and the equipping of your ministry through the gifts of the Holy Spirit (Romans 12:1-8; 1 Corinthians 12-14).

I pray all this for you, for the exaltation of Jesus Christ through the power of the Holy Spirit to the glory of the Father. Amen.

Seize the moment and walk in the Spirit today.

JOHN 17
PRAY LIKE JESUS!

Did you know that Jesus lived in a rhythm of intimacy with His Father through personal practices that strengthened His spiritual vitality? Jesus had a living faith, and His prayer life demonstrated that. In fact, John 17 is one of the most revealing chapters in the Gospels to learn how to pray like Jesus.

Jesus prays in John 17:1, 4-5, "Father, the hour has come; glorify Your Son, that the Son may glorify You, … I glorified You on the earth, having accomplished the work which You have given Me to do. Now, Father, glorify Me together with yourself, with the glory which I had with You before the world was."

Jesus models for us to pray for our own personal lives. Pray you would live your life in accordance to God's will and bring glory to His Name.

Jesus did not stop there because in verses 6-19, He prayed for His disciples. Jesus models for us to pray for those who are closest to us, and most intimately impacted by our lives, directly.

Jesus kept going; in verses 20-26, Jesus prayed for future generations of followers—that's us! Jesus teaches us to pray for people we will never meet or expect to personally impact, trusting God's faithfulness to all generations.

As you follow Jesus, may God's grace conform your life into the image of Jesus Christ as you learn to walk in the rhythms of intimacy with your Heavenly Father, just like Jesus.

Seize the moment and learn to pray like Jesus by following in His footsteps. He has prayed for you!

JOHN 18
THE SOURCE OF HOPE!

Where do you find your hope for the future?

John 18 confronts us with the weakness of man, the corruption of religion and government, and the fickleness of public opinion. This is a story about betrayal amongst friends, greed for power, the abuse of authority, and the weakness of human leadership. Jesus' crucifixion forever mocks our efforts to find hope in this world or in people.

Jesus did not despair and give up because He remained focused on His Father, the source of His hope. His eternal perspective gave Him the courage to do what needed to be done in the face of overwhelming evidence to despair. John 18:11 records Jesus saying to Peter, "Put the sword into the sheath; the cup which the Father has given Me, shall I not drink it?"

In other words: Don't panic! God has it under control; remain faithful! There is hope!

Listen to Jesus' eternal perspective as He went to the Cross. From John 18:36-37,

My kingdom is not of this world. If My kingdom were of this world, then My servants would be fighting so that I would not be handed over to the Jews; but as it is, My kingdom is not of this realm. … For this I have been born, and for this I have come into the world, to testify to the truth. Everyone who is of the truth hears My voice.

Seize the moment and find your hope in Jesus! Keep an eternal perspective because everything is not as it seems! Don't despair and don't give up! There is hope when you are looking to the Source of all hope! May His Kingdom come, His will be done, on Earth as it is in Heaven. Amen.

JOHN 19
FAITHFUL TO FAMILY RESPONSIBILITIES!

Would you consider yourself a responsible person? Do you find yourself going through circumstances that distract you from your most important responsibilities? Are you caught in the spin cycle of the tyranny of the urgent?

In John 19:25-27, we see the depths of Jesus' love, and His faithfulness to His mother:

Therefore, the soldiers did these things. But standing by the cross of Jesus were His mother, and His mother's sister, Mary the wife of Clopas, and Mary Magdalene. When Jesus then saw His mother, and the disciple whom He loved standing nearby, He said to His mother, "Woman, behold, your son!" Then He said to the disciple, "Behold, your mother!" From that hour the disciple took her into his own household.

This is a very powerful moment in the life of Jesus. He died young for us. He was brutalized and betrayed, scandalized and scorned, crucified like a common criminal. In that last night and day of Jesus' life, He went through greater agony than most of us can even imagine. He did this all for us so that we can be forgiven of our sins and brought back into a right relationship with God—restored unto the family of God with God as our Father. Jesus did all this without forgetting His responsibility as the eldest son to His mother. In the last moments of His life, Jesus ensured that His best friend, John the Beloved, would carry on His responsibility for caring for her in her old age.

I think Jesus just took all of our excuses away for why we are too busy, or too important, or too anything to fulfill our family responsibilities. Whether you are in the season of caring for elderly parents, or raising children, let us follow Jesus' example and be faithful to our families and friends, and our church, and our community.

Seize the moment and be faithful.

JOHN 20
PEACE BE WITH YOU!

What is the good fruit of the resurrection of Jesus Christ?

Listen to a phrase that flowed from Jesus' resurrected lips as He went to His followers in those first days of His victory over death.

In John 20:19, "Peace be with you!"
In John 20:21, "Peace be with you!"
In John 20:26, "Peace be with you!"

Great things come in threes! In the same way that Jesus asked Peter if he loved Him three times in John 21, He says, "Peace be with you!" to His followers three times upon His resurrection. Maybe it is threefold to symbolize each day of His experience of death. Death has lost its sting! Peace be with you!

Jesus' resurrection is the promise of faith; it guarantees your freedom from sin, your victory in the face of defeat, and your security in the Father's embrace! Peace be with you!

Jesus' resurrection is the promise of hope that from death comes life, from ashes comes beauty, and with each morning's sunrise comes new mercies! Peace be with you!

Jesus' resurrection is the promise of love, which calls you to be a person of peace, a minister of reconciliation, a lover of God and people! Peace be with you!

"Blessed are the peacemakers, for they shall be called sons of God" (Matthew 5:9). Blessed are those who bring good news with them wherever they go. Peace be with you!

Do you believe in the resurrection of Jesus Christ? If so, here is the promise, and here is your daily choice: Peace be with you!

Seize the moment and rest in the promises of God! Walk in faith, hope, and love! May God's peace go with you.

JOHN 21
YOU FOLLOW ME!

Are you content to do what God asks of you, or are you distracted by what everyone else is doing around you?

I am convinced that many people are miserable because they are playing the comparison game. There is an old adage, "Comparison is the root of all discontentment." Contrast this with the Apostle Paul, who triumphantly said, "I have learned to be content in whatever circumstances I am" (Philippians 4:11).

Which one are you? It's a choice—a learned behavior!

If you are struggling with this, then you are in good company. So did Peter! John 21:19-22 reveals both Peter's struggle and Jesus' focus. Jesus had just restored Peter back to his place as a leader in the church and had given him grace upon grace for Peter's three denials: "[Jesus] said to him, 'Follow Me!' Peter, turning around, saw the disciple whom Jesus loved following them ... So Peter seeing him said to Jesus, 'Lord, and what about this man?' Jesus said to him, 'If I want him to remain until I come, what is that to you? You follow Me!'"

We get distracted by comparison, in and outside the church. Jesus wants to keep us focused on Him. How does Jesus want to keep us focused? It is not with busy work, or job descriptions, or heavy burdens, but through a personal relationship with Him. Never forget that "follow Me" is a grace-based invitation to personal relationship; it is Jesus' calling you to get back in His easy yoke and learn from Him.

Seize the moment and follow Jesus! Learn contentment by taking your eyes off everyone else and focus on Jesus!

ACTS

ACTS 1
THE ACTS OF THE HOLY SPIRIT!

What does a "successful" congregation look like?

For most Christians, the answer to that question means you have to turn to the fifth book of the New Testament: Acts of the Apostles.

Acts 1:14 records this about the New Testament Church: "These all with one mind were continually devoting themselves to prayer, along with the women, and Mary the mother of Jesus, and with His brothers."

Here is an Acts mark of congregational success: the members are in "one mind," which means that they were brought into agreement with one another. Something or someONE acted upon the members to bring them into agreement with one another!

Jesus prayed for us to have this unity in John 17. Take some time to read and reflect upon His prayer for us.

Did you know that no congregation can be of "one mind" without someONE acting upon us to bring us there?

And that ONE is not me (a pastor), or any man or group of people! In fact, we as people get in the way of being in "one mind" most of the time, demanding our ways as His ways and our thoughts as His thoughts. There is no greater and more destructive pride than spiritual pride.

For any congregation to have any chance of being successful, I think we should think differently about the book we call, the "Acts of the Apostles." It should be called the "Acts of the Holy Spirit." If we are going to be of "one mind" and fulfill Jesus' prayer of John 17 in our congregation, it will only be by the work of the Holy Spirit.

Seize the moment and be faithful to God. Get in one mind with God, then let Him get us in one mind with each other.

ACTS 2
OUR HERITAGE AND LEGACY!

I'm writing this on the Fourth of July holiday, which, in the USA, reminds us of our inheritance as a nation! But it is not only our heritage, it is our legacy.

This Acts 2 story is our inheritance as the Church of Jesus Christ! This is not only our heritage, but it, too, is our legacy. The legacy we are called to leave to our communities is the legacy of God's power, presence, and love being in their midst—God is with us! Immanuel!

Acts 2:42-47 says this about our heritage and legacy:

They were continually devoting themselves to the apostles' teaching and to fellowship, to the breaking of bread and to prayer. Everyone kept feeling a sense of awe; and many wonders and signs were taking place through the apostles. And all those who had believed were together and had all things in common; and they began selling their property and possessions and were sharing them with all, as anyone might have need. Day by day continuing with one mind in the temple, and breaking bread from house to house, they were taking their meals together with gladness and sincerity of heart, praising God and having favor with all the people. And the Lord was adding to their number day by day those who were being saved.

Are you a member of His Church? Never forget that the Church is more than a building and more than a community organization. If we have learned anything during the COVID-19 pandemic, it is that the building is not the Church; the people are the Church. You can't close the Church, because the Church is comprised of people who show the world that God is with us—His love, His presence, and His power—Immanuel! It is to be visible!

Seize the moment and be the Church of Jesus Christ.

ACTS 3
ALONG YOUR DAILY PATHS!

Do you believe there is work for you to do in the well-tread paths of your daily routines and lives?

Acts 3 tells the story of the healing of a man who has been begging at the temple gates for a very long time. Acts 3:1-2 sets up the story,

> Now Peter and John were going up to the temple at the ninth hour, the hour of prayer. And a man who had been lame from his mother's womb was being carried along, whom they used to set down every day at the gate of the temple which is called Beautiful, in order to beg alms of those who were entering the temple.

This story is peculiar to me because it sounds so ordinary, so every day, and that's the point.

This is a well-traveled path for the disciples; they were entering the temple as they had with Jesus many times before. Jesus has walked by this man probably multiple times without healing him. This man is over 40 years old (see reference to him in Acts 4:22), and he had been brought to this gate of the temple daily for years. Even in the places where Jesus' physical footprints were left there was still a work for the Church to do.

This is peculiar because for some reason this man has been overlooked for years until the day Peter's and John's eyes were opened to his situation (Acts 3:4).

Are the eyes of your heart, as well as your physical ears and eyes, open so that God can use you in a similar way in your everyday life? Look with fresh eyes for those people in your daily life who need a touch from Jesus. Who or what have you been blind to until now?

Seize the moment and ask God to open your eyes to opportunities in your everyday life, along your well-tread paths.

ACTS 4
THE POWER OF ANNOYANCE!

There is a lot to be annoyed about in the world, in our nations, and in our own lives. You probably can't watch the news, or go on social media, without being annoyed.

Did you know there is a lot of pent-up power in the emotion of annoyance?

Peter and John were arrested for preaching in the temple after they healed the man lame from birth, because the religious leaders felt "greatly annoyed" by their teaching and proclamation about Jesus' resurrection from the dead (Acts 4:1-2, ESV).

Interestingly, the Greek word, translated "greatly annoyed" is used only twice in the New Testament. The second occasion is in Acts 16:18 when Paul cast out the spirit of divination from the slave girl being used by her masters to make money fortune telling. Paul was "greatly annoyed" at the unclean spirit's tormenting of this girl, so he cast out the demon; this got Paul and Silas beaten and imprisoned by the Romans in Philippi.

The religious leaders were moved to take action against Paul's Holy Spirit activity of healing the man in Acts 4 with the same emotion of annoyance that moved Paul to take action against a demonic spirit's activity in Acts 16. Both times, the followers of Jesus end up in prison. Both times, God used their imprisonment to expand the work of the gospel and save souls!

The emotion of annoyance is in both stories—it is a human reality that fuels action. The question is: what kinds of words and actions does "annoyance" empower in you?

Seize the moment and align annoyance with faith. Love what God loves. Hate what God hates. Pray before you speak, before you act, before you post something on social media, before you hit send on that text or email.

ACTS 5
GOD IS AT WORK!

Is God at work in today's world?

Acts 5 is filled with God's direct activity in the church and through the Apostles. Acts 5:1-11 is the story of the "active wrath of God" against Ananias and Sapphira for lying to the Apostles about a financial gift they were giving to the early church.

The result of such an active and direct work of God was tangible in the church. As Acts 5:11 states, "Great fear came over the whole church, and over all who heard of these things."

The church needs a healthy dose of the fear of the Lord today, to wake those who sleep and to focus those who are distracted!

Is God at work in the world? Absolutely!

But today, we experience God through the "passive wrath of God" (as explained clearly in Romans 1:18-32), where God gives people over to the consequences of their actions. Here are some examples from my experiences in today's church world:

1. Hearts harden (meaning people become stubbornly stuck in their ways of life and thinking) when they will not repent of their sin.
2. Relationships are strained or broken causing strife in families and in churches when someone lies, steals, or cheats.
3. The light of Christ's glory is dimmed through people's lives when hypocrisy (a double-mindedness and divided loyalty of a person's life) is allowed to exist, fed by daily life choices.

God is merciful in His justice, slow in His anger, and patient in His judgments. Do not misinterpret God's grace for apathy (God is good and He cares!), withdrawal (God is with us and He knows!), or impotence (God is all powerful and He is at work!).

Is God at work in the world today? YES! Through His people!

Seize the moment and be the hands and feet of God's work in today's world.

ACTS 6
WE EACH MUST DO OUR PART!

Are you ready and willing to do your part in the church body?

Acts 6:4 is actually a very important verse to how I view my life and ministry. It frames my understanding of what God has called me to do.

Listen to Acts 6:2-4,

So the twelve summoned the congregation of the disciples and said, "It is not desirable for us to neglect the word of God in order to serve tables. Therefore, brethren, select from among you seven men of good reputation, full of the Spirit and of wisdom, whom we may put in charge of this task. But we will devote ourselves to prayer and to the ministry of the word."

When there were needs not being met in the congregation (Acts 6:1), the people went to the leaders. They, in turn, didn't drop their work to fix it; rather, they empowered members of the church to fix the situation. From Moses to today, God's people have learned that delegation is God's way, because one person is not capable of doing it all without being crushed by the expectations, demands, and responsibilities of so many people.

The Bible teaches that every individual member of the Body of Christ is equally called to do that which you have been gifted and graced to do (1 Corinthians 12). The leaders are commanded to empower and equip you in that work (Ephesians 4:11-16). We are better together! This is how the Church grows in depth and breadth; each individual member gets healthy and does his or her part.

Are you ready and willing to do your part in the body of Christ?

Seize the moment and do your part as a member of the body of Christ. Please start with prayer and let God show you your next step.

ACTS 7
HAPPY ENDINGS!

Earlier this week, my six-year-old was upset because there was someone being mean to the main character in her animated show. Everything was not "sunshine and cotton candy," and Willow was not happy. She, like most of us, wants only happy endings.

Stephen's life and death teaches us about happy endings. Acts 7:59-60 records his death, "They went on stoning Stephen as he called on the Lord and said, 'Lord Jesus, receive my spirit!' Then falling on his knees, he cried out with a loud voice, 'Lord, do not hold this sin against them!' Having said this, he fell asleep."

Stephen's death confronts us with this reality: Faithfulness to God doesn't obligate God to give us a life of "sunshine and cotton candy." There will be hardship and suffering, pain and death. Jesus told us this ahead of time.

We need to change our minds about how we define the "happy life," and what having a "happy ending" looks or feels like. Here's the point: As long as your happiness is at the center of your decision making, you can't have a happy ending.

Jesus promises to give you the fullness of His joy in this life, and the hope of His eternal relationship with God. For this, He invites us to be faithful to Him.

Stephen lived and died exactly as he would have wanted because he gave his life to Jesus before anyone took his life. Acts 7 is all about Stephen's faithfulness—Stephen did get his happy ending!

Until we believe this, we are left living on the treadmill of "sunshine and cotton candy" pursuits.

Seize the moment and join with Stephen in giving your life to Jesus. Live a faithful life!

ACTS 8
GOD USES ALL THINGS FOR HIS GLORY!

Can God use evil for good?

Acts 8 starts with Saul, the Pharisee who oversaw Stephen's murder, ravaging the Christians in Jerusalem. We read in Acts 8:1-3,

> And on that day a great persecution began against the church in Jerusalem, and they were all scattered throughout the regions of Judea and Samaria, except the apostles. Some devout men buried Stephen, and made loud lamentation over him. But Saul began ravaging the church, entering house after house, and dragging off men and women, he would put them in prison.

What good could come from a development like this?

My favorite Old Testament story is the story of the patriarch Joseph, found in Genesis 37-50. The story concludes in Genesis 50:20, with Joseph talking to his brothers, "As for you, you meant evil against me, but God meant it for good in order to bring about this present result, to preserve many people alive."

I love this story, and the many stories in the Old Testament that proclaim the same thread of truth—God uses real people, with real faith, in real history to bring about His great plans. God is sovereign. God is faithful and true! God can use anyone for plans that are far greater than any of us can understand in the moment. The key is for you to live with a faith perspective as you go about your day.

Do you trust God to work it all out even if you don't understand what is going on? That trust must become your way of life.

The good that came from Acts 8 was a great expansion of the Church out of Jerusalem. It was a time of great growth, and it happened quickly.

Seize the moment and be patient as God is working all things together for His glory! Don't panic—God is with us!

ACTS 9
YOU ARE A CHOSEN INSTRUMENT!

Are stories important?

Acts 9 contains the most popular conversion story in the New Testament; verses 1-31 is the story of Saul's conversion and the early days of His new life in Christ. Saul's name is changed to Paul, and many today refer to him as the Apostle Paul, or Saint Paul. Paul was God's "chosen instrument" to establish Christianity beyond the borders of Israel—from a Jewish nationalistic religion to a relationship with God, available to all in the world through the chosen One of God, Jesus of Nazareth, the Christ.

Paul was used by God. Acts 9:15-16 testifies of God's call on his life, "Go, for he is a chosen instrument of Mine, to bear My name before the Gentiles and kings and the sons of Israel; for I will show him how much he must suffer for My name's sake."

Have you heard the expression, "Saved to serve"? When you are saved, you are saved to serve the Lord's purposes—you, too, are a "chosen instrument" of God's.

Can God use you? Ephesians 2:10 testifies about each person who comes to Jesus in faith, "For we are His workmanship, created in Christ Jesus for good works, which God prepared beforehand so that we would walk in them."

Your story will be different than Paul's, but none the less important; your story is what God will use to point people to Jesus Christ.

Is your story important? Yes! God has a greater purpose than you can see for your story! All of your story is important. You never know how your life experiences will intersect with another person's life experiences.

Seize the moment and share your story with other people. Call someone today, because you have been blessed to be a blessing!

ACTS 10
ETERNAL INVESTMENTS!

Do you know that God sees you being generous when you help someone with your time, talents, or treasures?

Acts 10:3-4 demonstrates this, "About the ninth hour of the day he clearly saw in a vision an angel of God who had just come in and said to him, 'Cornelius!' And fixing his gaze on him and being much alarmed, he said, 'What is it, Lord?' And he said to him, 'Your prayers and alms have ascended as a memorial before God.'"

What did God see and remember about the Roman centurion Cornelius?

1. **Prayers.** Prayers are a form of worship to God, a way of invoking God's power and presence in your life, and in the lives of others. Prayers are a very intimate part of who you are. God hears what is coming from your heart, the center of who you are. The Bible teaches us that our prayers are kept before God continuously, like incense before His throne. They are eternal.

If you want to hit the bullseye with your life, learn to pray! What does your heart say to God in your prayer life?

2. **Alms.** Alms are when you give something of value to the needy, poor, or destitute. What you give can either be your time and services, or food and finances; regardless, it is going out of your way to help someone for no benefit to yourself. The Bible teaches us that God rewards a person for what is done in secret; in other words, we are rewarded for what is done to truly help others without any benefit or recognition to the giver.

Alms giving is often the way God answers our prayers. Who can you bless today?

Seize the moment and invest in eternity. What does God see and remember about you?

ACTS 11
FAITH AND GOD'S INDWELLING!

Barnabas was a man of great encouragement. He is the kind of friend we all need to have, and I hope we can each be this kind of friend for others. Barnabas is described in Acts 11:24 as "a good man, and full of the Holy Spirit and of faith. And considerable numbers were brought to the Lord."

God uses real people, with real faith, in real history to do great and mighty works for His glory. God can use your friendships!

Jesus taught the disciples in John 14:23, "If anyone loves Me, he will keep My word; and My Father will love him, and We will come to him and make Our abode with him." Faith and the indwelling of the Holy Spirit are paired together in the Bible. We see evidence of this promised indwelling in Barnabas' life.

Are you a person of faith? Is there evidence of God's Spirit being at work in and through you?

Seize the moment and be an encourager to someone today. Be a good friend who points people to Jesus.

ACTS 12
LISTEN TO THE VOICE OF GOD!

To whose voices are you listening?

Acts 12:21-24 contrasts a man's voice with God's voice,

On an appointed day Herod, having put on his royal apparel, took his seat on the rostrum and began delivering an address to them. The people kept crying out, "The voice of a god and not of a man!" And immediately an angel of the Lord struck him because he did not give God the glory, and he was eaten by worms and died. But the word of the Lord continued to grow and to be multiplied.

The people were listening to their political leader, King Herod, as if he was a savior and a god, rather than looking to God himself for their hope and salvation. Two thousand years later, the same thing is happening in America today; so many people are putting their hope in politicians and celebrity voices rather than in God. We are looking to our cultural elite to save us, when there is only one name on Earth that can save—the name of Jesus Christ!

There are a lot of voices speaking today. So many, in fact, that it sounds like a cacophony of dissonant blowhards. It is my hope that these daily devotions are reminding you to listen to the Spirit-empowered Word of God, alive and active in the world today, calling you to the gospel of Jesus Christ!

Are you being more influenced by the voices of people, or the voice of God?

I am inviting you to start again. Start reading your Bible again, start praying again, start attending your local church again. We need an active relationship with God in our daily and weekly rhythms of life! Today is the day!

Seize the moment and return your heart focus to God and listen for His voice.

ACTS 13
USING YOUR TIME!

Time is marching on! Are you doing something with the time you have, or are you just doing your time?

Acts 13:36 says this about King David, "For David, after he had served the purpose of God in his own generation, fell asleep, and was laid among his fathers and underwent decay."

My time, and your time, on Earth is limited by God's design. We have been blessed with the gift of boundaries in this life. Why? So that we will embrace the time we have and grow up into our purposes. Friends, let me be painfully honest with you: you do not grow up just because you do your time! Biblical maturity is about how you embrace your time to learn and grow in knowledge, wisdom, and stature with God and people (Luke 2:52). Maturity and time are linked together by how you use your time to fulfill the purpose of God in your own generation.

What has God called you to accomplish in your lifetime and in your generation? How are you using your time?

God is calling you to remember that He has a purpose for your life in Jesus Christ. Don't just do your time; make the most of every day!

We each must embrace the reality that a day is coming when we will be laid to rest. As Hebrews 9:27 promises, "It is appointed for men to die once and after this comes judgment."

When the time comes, will you be like David and be found to have served the purposes of God in your generation?

You only get one chance. Use your time for God's glory!

Seize the moment and redeem the time you have been given; every breath you have is a gift! Every minute is an opportunity to grow closer to God.

ACTS 14
THE ANTIDOTE TO POISONED MINDS!

Why is there is so much anger and strife in our world?

Listen to Acts 14:2, "But the unbelieving Jews stirred up the Gentiles and poisoned their minds against the brothers" (ESV).

This verse stopped me in my tracks. The Greek word translated "poisoned" carries malicious intent, as to harm or embitter someone. This group sought to turn all the other people against the gospel of Jesus; they aimed to assassinate the character of, and discredit, the believers. But the evil that animates such motivations won't stop at discredit; it must win, and it will destroy anything that opposes it.

Sound familiar? Not much has changed, because the same evil is at work in us today as has been for thousands of years. No amount of technological progress changes the real issue!

Paul explains this so clearly in Romans 8:6-7, "For the mind set on the flesh is death, but the mind set on the Spirit is life and peace, because the mind set on the flesh is hostile toward God; for it does not subject itself to the law of God, for it is not even able to do so."

This is the real issue hidden behind all human issues—this hostility that our flesh (ego, self-willed efforts) has against God's rightful claim on our lives. We belong to Him, but, until we give over the deed of ownership, we will fight Him, and everyone else, who doesn't accept our right to rule our own empire.

The gospel is that Jesus came to "put to death the enmity [hostility]" (Ephesians 2:13-16) and to bring us under God's sovereign rule, where we find peace and rest.

Seize the moment and choose to give God all rights of ownership. God's Spirit in you is the only antidote to the poison that brings hostility between us all.

ACTS 15
EASY YOKE VS. HEAVY YOKES!

A biblical agricultural image for salvation is being in the yoke of God's covenant love.

Listen to Acts 15:8-11,

And God, who knows the heart, testified to them giving them the Holy Spirit, just as He also did to us; and He made no distinction between us and them, cleansing their hearts by faith. Now therefore why do you put God to the test by placing upon the neck of the disciples a yoke which neither our fathers nor we have been able to bear? But we believe that we are saved through the grace of the Lord Jesus, in the same way as they also are.

The earliest church council rejected circumcision, dietary laws, and Levitical Law adherence for a person to be saved and to be a part of the earliest church. So, what did they say saved a person?

Was it any kind of action a person must take? Was it baptism? Was it speaking in tongues? Was it a sacramental act of the church? No, in fact they refuted such ideas by saying, "why are you putting God to the test by placing a yoke on the neck of the disciples?" The yoke they were specifically referencing was the Levitical Law observance, but the principle applies to any form of religious legalism or self-righteous spirituality.

We have been saved by God's grace—the easy yoke of Jesus Christ (Matthew 11:28-30)!

Paul wrote in Galatians 5:1, "It was for freedom that Christ set us free; therefore keep standing firm and do not be subject again to a yoke of slavery."

Seize the moment and get in the only yoke that brings rest to your soul. You will know because the burden of His yoke is light, whereas, the burden of any other yoke is heavy!

ACTS 16
YOUR FAITH LEGACY IS PEOPLE!

To whom are you passing on your faith? Who is your faith legacy?

In Acts 16:1-5, Paul welcomes Timothy to the mission team, and "the churches were being strengthened in the faith, and were increasing in number daily" (5).

Later, in verses 6-15, Paul was invited in a vision by "a man of Macedonia" to the city of Philippi (9). There, Lydia and her household were saved, and she opened her home to the church.

Then, in verses 26-34, Paul and Silas are put in jail; shortly afterward, there's an earthquake, and, as a result, the despondent Philippi jailer and his family are saved.

The jailer asked Paul in verse 30, "What must I do to be saved?"

In accordance with the Jerusalem Council's decision in Acts 15, Paul replied simply in verse 31, "Believe in the Lord Jesus, and you will be saved, you and your household."

Paul is in uncharted territory. He has been asked to build churches where there has never been a church. Paul was able to travel through a large area bringing people to Christ, finding homes for the gatherings to occur, and appointing elders to oversee the continuing work of God in his absence (Acts 14:23).

The key was that Paul knew that he had to pass on his faith in Jesus Christ and empower other people to lead the ministries in his absence. Paul knew that at the heart of the Christian faith was the responsibility of passing on to other reliable people what had been given to Him (2 Timothy 2:2).

It's time for you to name names—In whom are you investing? Who will carry on your ministry?

Seize the moment and realize that the days are short. Who will carry on the faith because of your spiritual friendship? Who is your faith legacy?

ACTS 17
BE NOBLE LIKE A BEREAN!

Have you heard someone say, "be noble like a Berean," and wondered to yourself, what in world that even means?

Acts 17:10-11 explains what it means:

The brethren immediately sent Paul and Silas away by night to Berea, and when they arrived, they went into the synagogue of the Jews. Now these were more noble-minded than those in Thessalonica, for they received the word with great eagerness, examining the Scriptures daily to see whether these things were so.

Berea is a town in Macedonia; their citizens are called Bereans. As the Jewish people of Berea listened to Paul's teaching, the Bible says they "received the word with great eagerness" (11), which means they listened with an honest and sincere heart to understand Paul's teaching. Next, the Bereans did not just accept or deny what he said, but they, "[examined] the Scriptures daily to see whether these things were so" (11).

To be "noble like a Berean" requires two things:

1. You need good listening or reading skills so you can actually understand what the person is trying to communicate. Be respectful enough to hear them out and work through the material. Don't jump to conclusions and don't take things out of context. This requires love and humility, which is only possible when you are walking in the Spirit.
2. You need to have a good working knowledge of God's Word. This means that you will take the time to study your Bible, examine the Scriptures, and be able to apply the plumb line (standard) of God's Word to what you have read or listened to. This requires Bible time, not internet search time.

Seize the moment and start good life habits today by spending time with God every day in the Word and prayer. This is the only way to become gentle and humble like Jesus and discerning and wise with the Word.

ACTS 18
BLOOM WHERE YOU ARE PLANTED!

Are you blooming where you have been planted?

Acts 18:1-4 introduces a ministry couple:

After these things he left Athens and went to Corinth. And he found a Jew named Aquila, a native of Pontus, having recently come from Italy with his wife Priscilla, because Claudius had commanded all the Jews to leave Rome. He came to them, and because he was of the same trade, he stayed with them and they were working, for by trade they were tent-makers. And he was reasoning in the synagogue every Sabbath and trying to persuade Jews and Greeks.

Because of a government edict, this mature ministry couple (Priscilla and Aquila) were forced to go to Corinth. How did this mature ministry couple respond to their heartbreak?

We see, in verse 18 that Paul took Priscilla and Aquila with him after his 18 months in Corinth. Then in verse 19, Paul left them in Ephesus. Why? Was this salt in their open wound?

No! Paul entrusted to them the mentorship of a gifted new brother, Apollos. According to Acts 18:24-28, Apollos had a huge hole in the gospel he proclaimed—he only knew about the baptism of John.

So, what is a mature ministry couple to do? Are they to feel sorry for themselves because they are not in Rome anymore, or because they feel abandoned by Paul who left them in a strange place? No, self-pity would have shelved them for sure!

They bloomed where they were planted and started working with Apollos (Acts 18:26).

Did God effectively use Priscilla and Aquila? Yes! This couple was handpicked by God to mentor the Billy Graham of their day, leading to a dynamic growth of the gospel through Apollos (Acts 19; 1 Corinthians 3:6).

Seize the moment and trust God enough to bloom where you have been planted!

ACTS 19
WALK IN JESUS' AUTHORITY!

Do you walk in the authority of Jesus Christ?

Listen to Acts 19:13-16,

But also some of the Jewish exorcists, who went from place to place, attempted to name over those who had the evil spirits the name of the Lord Jesus, saying, "I adjure you by Jesus whom Paul preaches." Seven sons of one Sceva, a Jewish chief priest, were doing this. And the evil spirit answered and said to them, "I recognize Jesus, and I know about Paul, but who are you?" And the man, in whom was the evil spirit, leaped on them and subdued all of them and overpowered them, so that they fled out of that house naked and wounded.

Did you hear this quote: "I recognize Jesus, and I know about Paul, but who are you?"

Who are you? This is not a question of notoriety or familiarity, like you're not famous or important enough for me to recognize you. Rather, this is a statement of authority!

These exorcists were not authorized agents to wield the name that is above all names, the name by which all knees must bow. They were famous, but not authorized! These seven sons of Sceva remind us that the popularity on earth does not determine your spiritual authority in Heaven, which can only come from being in His name through a personal relationship with Jesus.

Don't be discouraged by the evil that is at work in the world; it will not win the day. That's God's promise! Rather, be encouraged that your name is written in the Lamb's book of life, and you have authority from God to shine His light that will pierce the darkness.

Seize the moment during the dark days. Remain humble of heart, confess Christ with your lips, put on the full armor of God, and keep your eyes fixed on Jesus. Walk in His authority!

ACTS 20
CONSTRAINED BY THE SPIRIT!

How do you determine the next steps of your life?

Paul was discerning his next steps in Acts 20:22-23, "And now, behold, I am going to Jerusalem, constrained by the Spirit, not knowing what will happen to me there, except that the Holy Spirit testifies to me in every city that imprisonment and afflictions await me" (ESV).

The Lord revealed to Paul that in every city ahead of him imprisonment and suffering await him. How could Paul have used this information?

He could have said, "Thanks for giving me the heads-up God, for protecting me by warning me ahead of time." But Paul didn't respond this way!

There is a key phrase that we need to focus on to understand Paul's decision; otherwise, we may attribute it to some kind of bravado or human motive. Paul said, "I am going to Jerusalem, constrained by the Spirit."

To be "constrained by the Spirit" is when you know intellectually that you have freedom to choose to do something or not, but you are overwhelmingly convinced, and unwaveringly determined, that this is what God would have you do!

The only way to know the work of the Holy Spirit is by investing time into your relationship with God through lots of time with Jesus—learning the way and voice of your Good Shepherd.

An essential way to know the difference between your own stubbornness or bravado and being constrained by the Spirit is this: what God has you to do will always align with His Word, His character, and His revealed plan to use the body of Christ to bring glory to Himself through the exaltation of Jesus Christ.

Seize the moment and ask God to be a part of your decision-making process. Spend time with Him so that you can discern the difference between His voice and all other voices.

ACTS 21
PRAY FOR RESOLVE!

After having received an admonition not to return to Jerusalem in Acts 21:4, Paul receives a dramatic and direct prophetic message in verses 10-14,

As we were staying there for some days, a prophet named Agabus came down from Judea. And coming to us, he took Paul's belt and bound his own feet and hands, and said, "This is what the Holy Spirit says: 'In this way the Jews at Jerusalem will bind the man who owns this belt and deliver him into the hands of the Gentiles.'" When we had heard this, we as well as the local residents began begging him not to go up to Jerusalem. Then Paul answered, "What are you doing, weeping and breaking my heart? For I am ready not only to be bound, but even to die at Jerusalem for the name of the Lord Jesus." And since he would not be persuaded, we fell silent, remarking, "The will of the Lord be done!"

So, what is going on in this story? Agabus' prophetic sign and message is recorded in the book of Acts as accurate, from God. The problem is not in verse 11 (the giving of the prophetic word and sign), but in verse 12; the friends and travel companions of Paul put their desire for his well-being and safety above God's will for his life. They misapplied the reason God gave it the prophetic word to Paul, and to them.

God gave this prophetic word to Paul to focus his mind and heart on doing God's will—to call Paul deeper in counting the cost of his mission, and to strengthen his resolve.

Seize the moment and ask God to give you the resolve to do His will. Pray that we all would have the resolve to follow Jesus faithfully in the most difficult days.

ACTS 22
LOVE ALL THE PEOPLES!

When does nationalism go too far?

Nationalism is comprised of patriotic feelings, principles, and efforts. Nationalism can take an extreme form, which is especially marked by a feeling of superiority over other countries.

This extreme form of nationalism says, "we are better than you." When this extreme form of nationalism is merged with religion you neither have a healthy form of patriotism, nor a humble practice of religion; rather, you have an ideology propelled by rocket fuel.

It is this kind of ideology that caused the Jewish people in Acts 22:22 to cry out about Paul, "Away with such a fellow from the earth, for he should not be allowed to live!" That's crazy talk!

They wanted to kill Paul because he was bringing the fulfilled hope of Judaism to non-Jewish people (the Gentiles). Even though their own Jewish scriptures say that the Jews would be a blessing to all people on Earth, and a light to the Gentiles, their ideology caused them to violently oppose the work of God. They wanted God to raise up a nationalistic kingdom on Earth, not a spiritual one that welcomes all nations, tribes, and people groups!

The same thing is happening today in American Christianity! The nation you are born into is where God birthed you in real time and in real history. Yes, we are to be good citizens and pray for our leaders—that is healthy patriotism. But we must not allow our nationalism to become compromised as an extreme form of prejudice against those to whom God has called us to bring the love of Jesus Christ.

Are you willing to be used by God to reach all peoples, to the ends of the Earth?

Seize the moment and invite God to search your heart for any feelings of prejudice or superiority that would limit who you are willing to love as your neighbor.

ACTS 23
CHOOSE YOUR LOYALTIES WISELY!

Our loyalties determine what we think about and how we conduct ourselves. What loyalties are influencing you?

This very personal question jumped out of the story in Acts 23 when Paul was on trial in the Sanhedrin, the Jewish court. Listen to Acts 23:6-10,

> But perceiving that one group were Sadducees and the other Pharisees, Paul began crying out in the Council, "Brethren, I am a Pharisee, a son of Pharisees; I am on trial for the hope and resurrection of the dead!" As he said this, there occurred a dissension between the Pharisees and Sadducees, and the assembly was divided. For the Sadducees say that there is no resurrection, nor an angel, nor a spirit, but the Pharisees acknowledge them all. And there occurred a great uproar; and some of the scribes of the Pharisaic party stood up and began to argue heatedly, saying, "We find nothing wrong with this man; suppose a spirit or an angel has spoken to him?" And as a great dissension was developing, the commander was afraid Paul would be torn to pieces by them and ordered the troops to go down and take him away from them by force, and bring him into the barracks.

Paul knew the true loyalties of the religious elites and exposed them for who they were—political parties interested in defending their positions of power. They were not living as humble followers of God, seeking to know Him first and foremost, discerning His will for those who trusted them to lead them spiritually through Word and prayer.

Paul remained free of all this and was at peace because of it!

I choose to repent of any divided loyalties and return wholeheartedly to my first love, Jesus Christ! To whom or what are you choosing to focus your life?

Seize the moment and check your loyalties. In Christ, you will have peace and rest.

ACTS 24
AN INVITATION TO INTIMACY WITH GOD!

Does it ever feel like life is going off course?

As we turn to the final chapters of the book of Acts, we find Paul making his way to Rome, just as God promised, but in the least likely of ways—as a prisoner!

In Acts 24:27 we see just how long Paul stayed in Caesarea alone, "But after two years had passed, Felix was succeeded by Porcius Festus, and wishing to do the Jews a favor, Felix left Paul imprisoned." That's over two years in a prison cell waiting! Ruler by ruler would examine Paul, and, like with Jesus, the rulers find no fault with him. But, in the name of politics and self-preservation, Paul would be kept in prison and on the slow winding path to Rome.

Where was God? Where was His promise?

The great people of God have always been formed in their faith and character through seasons of waiting and wandering: Abraham and the patriarchs, Joseph, Moses, King David . . . the list of faithful people forged in the fires of life's circumstances is long and all-encompassing!

This is the way of God, and this is the way of maturing in faith and character. What appears to be a long, slow, drawn-out, twisted journey from our perspective, is really a straight line to the heart of God.

God is not focused on efficiency; rather, God's aim is for intimacy!

So, what are you to do right now as myriad circumstances are wearing everyone thin and causing people to act out of fear and anxiety?

TRUST GOD! God is calling you to press into your relationship with Him. How will you see the events of this season of your life as an invitation to intimacy with God?

Seize the moment and grow closer to Jesus today. He is inviting you personally!

ACTS 25
THE RIPPLE EFFECT OF FAITH!

Have you ever thrown a tiny pebble in a pond and then watched the ripples go out from that small action? It's called a "ripple effect," and how we respond to our situations can cause a similar reaction.

In Acts 25, Paul is caught in a very difficult situation. Paul states in verses 10-11,

> I am standing before Caesar's tribunal, where I ought to be tried. I have done no wrong to the Jews, as you also very well know. If, then, I am a wrongdoer and have committed anything worthy of death, I do not refuse to die; but if none of those things is true of which these men accuse me, no one can hand me over to them. I appeal to Caesar.

The historical situation is complex, but Paul's response is faithful to God's mission for His life: to be Christ's witness to the Roman Empire.

Paul models for us three ways we can put courage into our hearts and remain faithful to God in hard situations, even under the stress of our own suffering and death.

1. **Paul anchors himself in the Word of God.** We, too, can memorize and meditate upon the Word of God to focus our courage and strength on faithful living.
2. **Paul believed in the power of prayer.** We, too, can pray for one another and ask others to pray for us. There is a deep comfort and peace that comes from knowing others are praying for you.
3. **Paul knew there was a bigger purpose for what he was going through.** Jesus told him that he was "a chosen instrument." We, too, are chosen instruments; we are called ambassadors for Christ.

Seize the moment and send out a ripple effect in your stressful situations today.

ACTS 26
THE CHURCH OF JESUS CHRIST!

What is the Church?

It is very important to see how Paul first learned about the church. Pay attention to this specific detail from his conversion story from Acts 26:14-15 (also found in Acts 9:4-5 and Acts 22:7-8), "And when we had all fallen to the ground, I heard a voice saying to me in the Hebrew dialect, 'Saul, Saul, why are you persecuting Me? It is hard for you to kick against the goads.' And I said, 'Who are you, Lord?' And the Lord said, 'I am Jesus whom you are persecuting.'"

Did you hear Jesus' question to Paul, "Why are you persecuting me?"

This is a significant question because it is Jesus' witness to what the Church is, from His perspective. When Paul persecuted the Church and the followers of the Way, Jesus made no distinction between Paul opposing Him personally and opposing the people. Jesus sees His Church as an extension of Himself!

This is illuminating insight into the mind of God. Is the Church just another organization in town, or is there something more to the Church?

Honestly, many pastors and church leaders have forgotten this and have become shop keepers—managing spreadsheets of their religious goods and caring more about their storefront appearances and marketing strategies than living incarnate lives! We must return to who we are as the Church by returning, each of us, to our first love!

The Church is the collective body of Christ on Earth. We are the incarnate witnesses of Jesus' gospel to all peoples. We are a holy (set apart) people declaring a coming Kingdom that is not yet in its fullness!

Seize the moment and be a healthy functioning member of Jesus' body on Earth! You are called to be so much more than a member of an organization. We are so much more.

ACTS 27
TAKE COURAGE IN THE STORM!

Several years ago, during the relief efforts after a massive tornado ripped through Henryville, Indiana, a billboard went up declaring, "Don't tell your God how big your storm is, tell your storm how big your God is!"

In Acts 27, Paul, a prisoner in chains, was on his way to Rome. He was on a boat with 276 people when a bad decision was made to keep pressing on into the storm season. They were now approaching their fourteenth day of a horrifying storm experience. Everyone's life was in danger, and people were hungry and scared, when Paul stood up and spoke to the people in Acts 27:22-26:

> Yet now I urge you to keep up your courage, for there will be no loss of life among you, but only of the ship. For this very night an angel of the God to whom I belong and whom I serve stood before me, saying, "Do not be afraid, Paul; you must stand before Caesar; and behold, God has granted you all those who are sailing with you." Therefore, keep up your courage, men, for I believe God that it will turn out exactly as I have been told. But we must run aground on a certain island.

There are many storms in our lives. In addition to whatever you are going through personally, at home, or at work, our communities and nation are going through a stormy season.

Unlike Paul, I have not received a message from an angel for you, but I do have Jesus' words hidden in my heart: "In the world you have tribulation, but take courage; I have overcome the world" (John 16:33b).

Seize the moment and take courage in this storm—for Jesus has overcome the world.

ACTS 28
OPEN-ENDED ENDINGS!

Years ago, I remember going to see *The Fellowship of the Ring* at the movies, and, after three hours of storytelling, it just ended. In fact, it ended right where the book stopped. Half of the people booed, and the other half clapped.

Why? Because the movie was the first part of an ongoing story; it left you literally looking out at what was ahead instead of nicely packaging what was behind. It was an open-ended ending.

The same is true in the last chapter of the book of Acts. Listen to Acts 28:30-31, the last two verses, "And [Paul] stayed two full years in his own rented quarters and was welcoming all who came to him, preaching the kingdom of God and teaching concerning the Lord Jesus Christ with all openness, unhindered."

Paul was still a prisoner in Rome, and we don't get to see what happens next.

Why? Because the story was never about Paul, just like the story is never about us. Each of our lives will have an open-ended ending because this life is not all that we have. Our lives are about pointing to a larger story that will never end—the story of God!

By the way, I was one of the people who clapped when I went to see *The Fellowship of the Ring.*

Why? Simple—because I read the book, I wasn't surprised with its ending. In fact, I was happy it ended incomplete because I knew the best was yet to come!

Seize the moment and look at what is ahead of you. Can you see with the eyes of faith an eternal horizon, or is your sight bound up with this short life? There is no ending to your story in God, only new beginnings.

ROMANS

ROMANS 1
FAITHFULNESS IS A DECISION WE MAKE!

Why is it that so many people struggle with the concepts of obligation or duty when it comes to their relationship with Jesus? For example, we often say, don't give out of duty, but give out of a thankful heart. But can't a thankful heart lead to a commitment to give faithfully, sacrificially, and systematically? Why separate the concepts?

This is so important in our marriages and with our children. We love them; therefore, we commit to act towards them in a certain way—we obligate ourselves to the highest of virtues and values for the sake of our family's well-being. Not doing so is to mock our proclaimed love!

Paul understood this and expressed his sense of duty to go to Rome, stating in Romans 1:14-15, "I am under obligation both to Greeks and to barbarians, both to the wise and to the foolish. So, for my part, I am eager to preach the gospel to you also who are in Rome."

Paul gives us five reasons why he made the decision to obligate himself to get to Rome:

1. **Thankfulness!** Their world-wide testimony of faith moved his heart (8).
2. **Prayer!** His unceasing prayer for them solidified his conviction to go (9-10).
3. **Impartation!** He wanted to empower and equip them in their ministry (11).
4. **Encouragement!** He desired to be mutually encouraged by their faith (12).
5. **Mission!** He knew a great harvest was going to happen in Rome and he wanted to be a part of it (13-15).

Seize the moment and be faithful to the God you love by making decisions that obligate you to act according to what you know is true—even when you don't feel like it!

ROMANS 2
A LEVEL PLAYING FIELD!

Do we play on a level playing field?

When I was training for the Olympics, I felt the pressure that comes with elite sports to "level the playing field." I had previously attempted to make the team and had missed; I was so hungry to make the team, that I lost perspective—I became consumed by my own ambition.

Have you ever been consumed by a passion? Have you ever lost perspective on what really matters in life?

Romans 2:4-8 gives us a sober assessment to keep us focused with an eternal perspective:

> Or do you think lightly of the riches of His kindness and tolerance and patience, not knowing that the kindness of God leads you to repentance? But because of your stubbornness and unrepentant heart you are storing up wrath for yourself in the day of wrath and revelation of the righteous judgment of God, who will render to each person according to his deeds: to those who by perseverance in doing good seek for glory and honor and immortality, eternal life; but to those who are selfishly ambitious and do not obey the truth, but obey unrighteousness, wrath and indignation.

The sad truth is that I forget my own story sometimes. Then, because God is merciful, He reminds me again of my great need. He calls me back to Him, the Holy and Sovereign God, who is patient with judgement and generous with His covenant love.

Seize the moment and remember from what you have been saved! Don't let pride or ambition get ahold of your heart; remain humble towards yourself and other people. Truly, the playing field is already level. Each of us deserves judgment for our sin and we all must learn to live in daily dependence on God's mercy and grace. Never forget!

ROMANS 3
DIGGING DEEP INTO GOD'S WORD!

Paul's writings, starting with Romans, invite us to become students of the Bible. Unlike the storytelling of the Gospels and Acts, Romans is a theological treatise of the gospel, and it takes some work to mine the depths of it.

For example, listen to Romans 3:21-25a,

But now apart from the Law the righteousness of God has been manifested, being witnessed by the Law and the Prophets, even the righteousness of God through faith in Jesus Christ for all those who believe; for there is no distinction; for all have sinned and fall short of the glory of God, being justified as a gift by His grace through the redemption which is in Christ Jesus; whom God displayed publicly as a propitiation in His blood through faith.

This is a very important Scripture passage as Paul is laying out the truths that lead us to understand our need for Jesus Christ and how we can be saved.

This short section from Romans 3 is loaded with biblical concepts and vocabulary that will require you to be a serious student of the Bible if you want to get the most out of it.

Here are three practical steps you can take to becoming a responsible student of God's Word:

1. Submit your reading time to God by praying before you read. You need the Holy Spirit to teach you, to guide you into all truth.
2. Resist the enemy of your soul who wants to distract you from reading your Bible. If he can't stop you from reading it, he will seek to distract you from understanding and applying it.
3. Study the Word of God. Don't just read over the surface, dig into it! Pull out a journal, use a Bible dictionary, and get serious about your Bible study time.

Seize the moment and dig deep into God's Word today.

ROMANS 4
DO NOT WAVER ... PRESS ON!

I graduated from the U.S. Army's Ranger School in 1997. One of the many ways they tried to break us was by physically and mentally pushing people past the finish line. For example, you think you are going for a five-mile run, but they keep pushing you farther. Why? To see if you have the fortitude to press on!

Today is the five-month anniversary of the COVID-19 pandemic impacting our small community. On this day five months ago, I sat with a group of pastors, and our county health department, and we all realized the sacrificial teamwork that would be required of our community leaders to prevent our local health care systems from being overwhelmed. Today, like in Ranger School, we are at the five-mile mark; people are tired, frustrated, and are beyond ready to be done—but we must keep going.

Do we have the fortitude to press on?

We read in Romans 4:19-22,

Without becoming weak in faith [Abraham] contemplated his own body, now as good as dead since he was about a hundred years old, and the deadness of Sarah's womb; yet, with respect to the promise of God, he did not waver in unbelief but grew strong in faith, giving glory to God, and being fully assured that what God had promised, He was able also to perform. Therefore, it was also credited to him as righteousness.

Abraham did not waver in God's promises! He had every reason to stop trying, to quit, but He didn't. He kept His faith and pressed on! Friends, don't lose hope; God is not done yet. We may not know how much further ahead the finish line is, but with God all things are possible.

Seize the moment and do not waver in your faith! God's got this ... Press on!

ROMANS 5
MESSY CHURCH!

Are you willing to let your church become a messy church?

I'm not talking about the bathrooms, or the building, or landscape management. I'm talking about the church! Examine Romans 5:6-8 closely, "For while we were still weak, at the right time Christ died for the ungodly. For one will scarcely die for a righteous person—though perhaps for a good person one would dare even to die—but God shows his love for us in that while we were still sinners, Christ died for us."

Did you know that fishermen don't catch clean fish? If we are to be "fishers" of men and women (Mark 1:17), then we must realize that, just like with catching fish, people are caught dirty ("while we were yet sinners," as in Romans 5:8).

Now, you can go to a restaurant and pay good money for the professionals to serve you up a cleaned and well-prepared fish in a beautiful environment, but I guarantee somewhere along the line someone caught that fish while it was still dirty from swimming in its natural habitat. That fisherman had to be willing to get dirty himself to catch that fish.

Churches should be more like the fisherman's humble shack than the patron's pristine restaurant!

Every person that Jesus Christ died for is still dirty with sin when the Holy Spirit leads them to a church gathering! The only place that will be a beautiful pristine restaurant with perfectly prepared fish is Heaven, when all the family of God will be face-to-face with Jesus Christ. Glory to God!

Until that Day, we should expect messy.

Seize the moment and let's get messy for the Kingdom of God!

ROMANS 6
FREE FROM SHAME!

Shame is a powerful emotion! It can be demoralizing, debilitating, and destructive when it gets a choke hold on your soul. It is defined as "a painful emotion caused by consciousness of guilt, shortcoming, or impropriety; a condition of humiliating disgrace or disrepute; something that brings censure or reproach."

Do you want to be set free from feelings of shame?

I want you to be free from shame! More importantly, God wants you to be free!

Romans 6:20-23 describes,

For when you were slaves of sin, you were free in regard to righteousness. Therefore what benefit were you then deriving from the things of which you are now ashamed? For the outcome of those things is death. But now having been freed from sin and enslaved to God, you derive your benefit, resulting in sanctification, and the outcome, eternal life. For the wages of sin is death, but the free gift of God is eternal life in Christ Jesus our Lord.

Shame is a real condition between you and God that is caused by your sin and experienced in the truest depths of your soul! It is a manifestation of the enmity—the strife—between you and God.

For this very reason Jesus came—to remove the conflict between you and God—to restore you back into a right relationship with Him!

On the Cross of Calvary, Jesus Christ took the death you deserve for your sin that manifests these feelings of shame in your soul. Through faith in Jesus—true confession and repentance of sin—you are no longer a "slave to sin," meaning you have been rescued from the vicious soul cycle caused by unconfessed sin.

Jesus wants you to live free from sin and fully alive in God's peace.

Seize the moment and bring all of your sin, shame, and remorse to the throne of grace.

ROMANS 7
POWER OVER THE SIN NATURE!

Have you ever asked yourself, "Why did I do that?"

Paul did! Paul wrote in Romans 7:15, "For what I am doing, I do not understand; for I am not practicing what I would like to do, but I am doing the very thing I hate."

We have a choice at those moments: either look for blame outside of ourselves (play the blame game) or take personal responsibility for what we have done or said.

What do you do? Do you blame your upbringing, or the society around you? Do you blame your Creator for making you that way? Are you always finding reasons to blame someone (anyone) outside of yourself?

If so, you are not free in Christ! You are bound up in your sin nature which seeks, above all, to remain hidden, but in control.

The key is to take responsibility of your personal agency and be set free from the sin nature. Just read Romans 7 to learn more.

We are not victims! God did not leave us powerless!

The next time you are feeling seduced by the philosophies of this world to blame someone else or some situation for your sin, just go straight to Jesus Christ and ask for forgiveness for your sin. He is ready and willing to forgive you so run quickly to His throne of grace with confidence.

Seize the moment: Don't delay! Don't debate! Don't rationalize! Just run into His embrace and find grace! I promise you that this honest decision and act of humility will save you a world of heartache. In fact, it will change your whole life! Asking forgiveness is a daily way to find freedom and experience peace and rest in the Lord's loving embrace.

ROMANS 8
SETTING YOUR LIFE ON THE SPIRIT!

Who or what influences your heart and mind?

There is an old Cherokee proverb of two wolves fighting. Each wolf represents something within the person: one the evil a person can do and the other the good. Which one wins? The one you feed!

Listen to Paul in Romans 8:5-8,

For those who are according to the flesh set their minds on the things of the flesh, but those who are according to the Spirit, the things of the Spirit. For the mind set on the flesh is death, but the mind set on the Spirit is life and peace, because the mind set on the flesh is hostile toward God; for it does not subject itself to the law of God, for it is not even able to do so, and those who are in the flesh cannot please God.

God's wisdom empowers the person's individual responsibility to choose how to live his or her own life.

Here are three practical tips on how you can do this on a daily basis:

1. Choose each day which wolf you will feed. May your first action be a prayer of dedication when you ask the Holy Spirit to superintend your day. Design the beginning of your day to set your mind and heart on God.
2. Throughout your day, capture moments to remind yourself of the Spirit's presence. Use your phone and technology wisely, set up tangible reminders, and find friends who can help.
3. Take care of yourself and eat healthy, make time for personal care, and get to bed on time so that you are well rested to start your next day in step. Feeding the Spirit includes taking care of your body; it is the "temple of the Holy Spirit" (1 Corinthians 6:19).

Seize the moment and set your mind and heart on the things of the Spirit throughout your day.

ROMANS 9
THE GRACE OF GOD'S CHOOSING!

It was 1991; my mom watched from the front door of my childhood home in South Windsor, Connecticut. There it was, the envelope from the admissions department of the United States Military Academy. I had walked through the arduous process of receiving a congressional nomination, had taken and re-taken standardized testing, and had made every effort to secure my appointment to West Point. When the letter came saying that I had been chosen, I raised up my arms in what was the greatest accomplishment of my life up to that point. As I celebrated, my mom cried tears of joy and pride. We had worked hard for me to be chosen to become a member of the Long Gray Line.

Now, fast forward to 2002: What a glorious day! I stood in the living room of that same house; I had been chosen again, this time not by any effort or merit, but by God's sovereign grace. My mom cried tears of joy and astonishment at the news. This time, with my wife on my arm, we stepped out in faith because we had been called to the pastorate and I was leaving my army career behind. It was by God's grace that we were taking steps toward seminary.

Paul illuminates God's work, and not our own, in His sovereign choosing. Here is a glimpse from Romans 9:20-21, "On the contrary, who are you, O man, who answers back to God? The thing molded will not say to the molder, 'Why did you make me like this,' will it? Or does not the potter have a right over the clay, to make from the same lump one vessel for honorable use and another for common use?"

Have you experienced the joy of being chosen by God's grace and not by your own works? Do you believe it is true, or are you still focusing upon what you can do to earn favor with God?

Seize the moment and find rest in what only God can do: rest in the grace of God's salvation!

ROMANS 10
KEEP THE WORD OF CHRIST FIRST!

We live in such a loud and fast world. How in the world are we expected to remain focused on what matters when so many agendas keep coming at us? What steps are you taking to keep first things first?

In Romans 10:17, Paul explains that "faith comes from hearing, and hearing by the word of Christ."

Are you hearing the word of Christ in your daily lives? How? Think about how you have or have not created effective rhythms of life that keep the word of Christ first in your day and before you throughout your day. If you are to remain faithful in today's loud world, you must find ways to do so.

Why? It has been said that to walk with Christ faithfully we must have the gospel preached to us daily. We are that easily distracted and overrun by the many messages bombarding us. We live in a loud world and God does not compete with it. His invitation has been made and the announcement has gone forth … Are you listening? Not just once upon a time, but today: Who are you listening to today?

Focus time and energy to listen attentively to the gospel of Jesus Christ. Draw close to God and He will draw close to you. That's His promise!

Seize the moment and keep the Word of Christ first in your life!

ROMANS 11
GOD'S GRACE TELLS A BETTER STORY!

Have you ever felt defeated and disqualified?

Paul begins Romans 11 with an Old Testament reminder of Elijah from 1 Kings 17-19. Paul teaches us that God's grace tells a better story in Romans 11:1-6:

> I say then, God has not rejected His people, has He? May it never be! For I too am an Israelite, a descendant of Abraham, of the tribe of Benjamin. God has not rejected His people whom He foreknew. Or do you not know what the Scripture says in the passage about Elijah, how he pleads with God against Israel? "Lord, they have killed Your prophets, they have torn down Your altars, and I alone am left, and they are seeking my life." But what is the divine response to him? "I have kept for Myself seven thousand men who have not bowed the knee to Baal." In the same way then, there has also come to be at the present time a remnant according to God's gracious choice. But if it is by grace, it is no longer on the basis of works, otherwise grace is no longer grace.

When Elijah was confronted by the qualifying grace of God, all of Elijah's perspectives of his own fears and failures were put aside by the overwhelming truth of God's perspective. But, if it had been up to Elijah, his story would have ended in 1 Kings 19:4. He said, "It is enough; now, O LORD, take my life, for I am not better than my fathers."

Has a twisted perspective of your situation ever caused you to feel like your story is finished?

I've been there! Allow me to tell you the conclusion I had to learn the hard way: God uses the worst places of our lives to do His best work; at our "rock-bottom," God's grace can become the dominant story line of our lives. And this is where God gets the glory!

Seize the moment and remain faithful through the hardship of your moment! Don't bail before the blessing!

ROMANS 12
FREEDOM FROM HATE AND BITTERNESS!

Have you ever wanted to strike back at someone? Have you ever been consumed with vengeance?

In Romans 12:17-21, Paul explains how we are called to live out the forgiveness of Jesus Christ towards other people,

> Never pay back evil for evil to anyone. Respect what is right in the sight of all men. If possible, so far as it depends on you, be at peace with all men. Never take your own revenge, beloved, but leave room for the wrath of God, for it is written, "Vengeance is Mine, I will repay," says the Lord. "But if your enemy is hungry, feed him, and if he is thirsty, give him a drink; for in so doing you will heap burning coals on his head." Do not be overcome by evil, but overcome evil with good.

This is a hard teaching for many of us! We can't do this on our own strength, but only by the Spirit.

Hate and bitterness are a poison that spreads quickly throughout our lives. There is only one antidote—forgiveness and grace! Entrusting the situation to God and trusting Him to bring vengeance and justice is the only way to find rest for your soul. You are called to live out your faith in an evil world by doing good!

How do you know when you have truly forgiven someone? When you can actively pray for their good and not their harm. When you want for them what God has given you—salvation and blessings.

Are you a person of blessings or of curses? Of forgiveness or grudges? One pathway leads to freedom, the other to slavery! Truly, what you do with your hate and bitterness is your choice today! Don't wait another minute—choose the pathway of forgiveness and grace!

Seize the moment and take active steps not only toward forgiving people today, but toward blessing them in the name of Jesus.

ROMANS 13
GOD'S KINGDOM IS A RELATIONAL KINGDOM!

The Apostle Paul focuses us on the crucial human need of our lives: relationships. As one of my old pastors, the Rev. Ren Wallen, used to say, "The Kingdom of God is a relational kingdom." It was the lens through which he not only saw the gospel, but also through which he called the church into obedience to the commandments of Jesus Christ.

Paul commands in Romans 13:8-10,

Owe nothing to anyone except to love one another; for he who loves his neighbor has fulfilled the law. For this, "You shall not commit adultery, You shall not murder, You shall not steal, You shall not covet," and if there is any other commandment, it is summed up in this saying, "You shall love your neighbor as yourself." Love does no wrong to a neighbor; therefore love is the fulfillment of the law.

Truly, our relationships on earth are the litmus test of our faith in Jesus Christ! In other words, how we love our neighbor tells us the truth about whether or not we truly love God.

What destroys our relationships?

Sin destroys relationships! Not being right with God leads to a distortion of what matters in our daily lives, and that puts pressure on our relationships (at home, or work, or church) to do more for us than they can possibly do, and that is a heavy burden that crushes them. People can never do for you what only Jesus can!

The health of your relationships tells you the truth about your faith in Jesus; the Kingdom of God is a relational kingdom!

Seize the moment and prioritize relationships starting with getting right in your #1 relationship with Jesus! Until you prioritize Him, you will be bound up in your sin nature's selfishness to use people for your own happiness. Only the Spirit can set us free to truly love as Christ first loved us!

ROMANS 14
FOCUS ON WHAT MATTERS MOST!

How do you remain focused on what is most important in life? Do you get caught up with things that, at the end of the day, miss the mark on what matters to God?

In Romans 14:17-19, Paul continues to teach us about how we are to live as citizens of Heaven on the earth, teaching, "For the kingdom of God is not eating and drinking, but righteousness and peace and joy in the Holy Spirit. For he who in this way serves Christ is acceptable to God and approved by men. So then we pursue the things which make for peace and the building up of one another."

It is so easy to focus on what is important to man and miss what matters to God! Paul teaches us that what matters to God is righteousness, peace, and joy in the Holy Spirit!

The Kingdom of God is from the inside out. The righteousness of God has been imputed on you! It is the work of the Holy Spirit to transform our lives through faith, not by works! Faith is a gift that must be received with humility.

The Kingdom of God is one that reconciles relationships, first vertically with God, then horizontally with one another. Peace is the presence of God in a broken world, through us; we have been called to be "ministers of reconciliation" (2 Corinthians 5:17-21).

The Kingdom of God exhibits the glory of God through joy; we are called to be joyful messengers. Jesus wants your life to be marked by the fullness of His joy (John 15:11). This is a true abiding joy that is anchored in us through the sealing and anointing work of the Holy Spirit.

Seize the moment and walk in God's sovereign grace. You are a citizen of Heaven, so learn the difference between what is important to God and what is important to man; then choose wisely how you shall live.

ROMANS 15
HOPE, HARMONY, AND HOSPITALITY!

The Christian life is marked by certain attributes clearly laid out for us in Scripture. Let's look at 3 H's found in Romans 15:4-7,

> For whatever was written in earlier times was written for our instruction, so that through perseverance and the encouragement of the Scriptures we might have hope. Now may the God who gives perseverance and encouragement grant you to be of the same mind with one another according to Christ Jesus, so that with one accord you may with one voice glorify the God and Father of our Lord Jesus Christ. Therefore, accept one another, just as Christ also accepted us to the glory of God.

How is your **Hope?** Hope is faith focused on the future. When we lose hope, we lose our ability to see God working in and through us to bring about His purposes for the future.

How is your **Harmony?** In Jesus, we become of the same mind. Harmony is the process of bringing together that which is diverse for a unified purpose. For followers of Christ, the purpose is to lift up the name of Jesus above all names so that all people came come and see what the Lord has done for them. In our diversity, we have unity in Jesus Christ!

How is your **Hospitality?** It is not about simple smiles and a facade of caring; hospitality involves accepting one another and truly meeting the needs of others. Christians are called to be the hands and feet of Christ with arms wide open and hands outstretched!

These 3 H's—hope, harmony, and hospitality—serve one purpose: to make the presence of God known in and through the Church—the body of Christ!

Seize the moment and respond to the presence of God through manifesting hope, harmony, and hospitality in your relationships.

ROMANS 16
BUILDING STRONG BRIDGES!

Do you know how to make strong bridges?

Listen to a couple quick excerpts from Romans 16:1-16:

- "I commend to you our sister Phoebe, who is a servant of the church" (1).
- "Greet Priscilla and Aquila, my fellow workers in Christ Jesus, who for my life risked their own necks" (3-4).
- "Greet Rufus, a choice man in the Lord, also his mother and mine" (13).

Do you hear Paul building strong bridges with the Romans?

What do I mean when I say that Paul is building bridges? Allow me to explain with a little story telling of my own.

At the end of 2009, my family transitioned from pastoral ministry in the Silicon Valley of northern California to pastoral ministry in the corn belt of east-central Indiana. Needless to say, when you move over 2,500 miles, from urban to rural, there will be some major cultural issues that have to be navigated, even when you speak the same language and are citizens of the same country.

Here are some things I remember that other people did to help our ministry and life in a new community start well. Like in Paul's letter to the Romans, before we even got here, people reached out to us. Then, we were welcomed to our new home when we drove into town, even with snow on the ground and icy streets. As we got moved in, whether it was meals or a leaky toilet, people were available to help us. We needed help and when it was extended to us, we received it thankfully. Because of that we knew we were loved and a part of a new family immediately!

How are you building bridges with people in our community? How about in our church? What are some practical steps you can take today to help someone feel like they are loved, welcomed, and wanted?

Seize the moment and take personal responsibility as a bridge builder to one person or one family today.

1 & 2 CORINTHIANS

1 CORINTHIANS 1
THE FAMILY OF GOD!

Did you know that the Church is called to be one big happy family? That sounds wonderful until you commit your life to actually bring it about.

All our families have problems—communication and conflict—so, just imagine how difficult it is being a big old healthy church family where many nuclear family dynamics contribute. Then, we are called to work through those issues together to have all things in common and, as Paul commands us in 1 Corinthians 1:10, to live with "no divisions among you, but that you be made complete in the same mind and in the same judgment."

True confessions? This is an impossible expectation from my experience! You want to talk about dysfunctional families, try putting dozens or hundreds of family units together. It's not just impossible, it's an insane social experiment!

Welcome to Paul's letters to the family of God located in ancient Corinth, which probably could have earned the honor of most dysfunctional family in the history of the New Testament. Listen to Paul start off the conversation with them in 1 Corinthians 1:26-29:

> For consider your calling, brethren, that there were not many wise according to the flesh, not many mighty, not many noble; but God has chosen the foolish things of the world to shame the wise, and God has chosen the weak things of the world to shame the things which are strong, and the base things of the world and the despised God has chosen, the things that are not, so that He may nullify the things that are, so that no man may boast before God.

Paul agreed with me: "IMPOSSIBLE!" Paul knew and taught the Corinthians, and I am teaching you today: what is impossible for us is possible for God!

When the Church lives up to God's commands, the world will see and give God glory!

Seize the moment and trust God to do the impossible in you and through you for His glory!

1 CORINTHIANS 2
THE GOODNESS OF THE MYSTERY!

Do you like a good mystery?

I enjoy a good suspenseful mystery novel. One of my favorite story tellers is a Christian author named Ted Dekker. The thing about reading a great author is that you learn their style and start finding the meaning behind the mystery; you can more easily see the insights along the way. You find small details that seem insignificant at first, but you learn to recognize them as keys to another layer of the story that has not yet been revealed.

The bottom line is, you start looking for the mystery everywhere because you believe the mystery is good!

The Apostle Paul speaks of the mystery of God throughout 1 Corinthians 2. Verse 7 overtly explains, "but we speak God's wisdom in a mystery, the hidden wisdom which God predestined before the ages to our glory."

Though there is much mystery in our lives and in what is happening in the world today and how God can possibly use it all for His purposes and to His glory, let me share with you the greatest mystery of all: you can know personally the ultimate Storyteller! The more you spend time getting to know Jesus Christ and listening over and over again to Him through His Word, the more your mind and heart are opened to the small details that seem insignificant at first, that we later learn are keys to another layer of the story that is still unfolding in us and through us.

Seize the moment and spend time with the great Storyteller. His mystery is good so trust Him with your story, so that every detail points to His Story! To God be the Glory!

1 CORINTHIANS 3
GOD'S FELLOW WORKERS!

Did you know that we are all in this together and not a single one of us is more important than another? We may have different gifts, callings, and responsibilities that we must stand before God to be held accountable for, but we each have great potential to make an eternal impact on our communities.

Paul wrote in 1 Corinthians 3:3-9,

> For since there is jealousy and strife among you, are you not fleshly, and are you not walking like mere men? For when one says, "I am of Paul," and another, "I am of Apollos," are you not mere men? What then is Apollos? And what is Paul? Servants through whom you believed, even as the Lord gave opportunity to each one. I planted, Apollos watered, but God was causing the growth. So then neither the one who plants nor the one who waters is anything, but God who causes the growth. Now he who plants and he who waters are one; but each will receive his own reward according to his own labor. For we are God's fellow workers; you are God's field, God's building.

This passage is for more than just the leaders of the church—it is for all of us! It is always about God and what God is doing through His people. We are called to be one unified body. We are God's fellow workers!

This means we are called to follow the example of Jesus Christ: Are you sacrificial in your love and forgiveness to others? Are you serving people in the name of Jesus Christ?

Seize the moment! Walk in step with the Spirit and you will find yourself in step with God's people. Remember, it is agreement with the Head of the Church—Jesus Christ—that causes the members of the body to walk in alignment with one another. Let us be God's fellow workers! For His glory!

1 CORINTHIANS 4
THE AIM OF APPRENTICESHIP IS LOVE!

If you want to become a master electrician, you must start as an apprentice. Every student needs a teacher. We all must learn from someone!

Paul explains his heart for this truth in 1 Corinthians 4:14-17,

I do not write these things to shame you, but to admonish you as my beloved children. For if you were to have countless tutors in Christ, yet you would not have many fathers, for in Christ Jesus I became your father through the gospel. Therefore I exhort you, be imitators of me. For this reason I have sent to you Timothy, who is my beloved and faithful child in the Lord, and he will remind you of my ways which are in Christ, just as I teach everywhere in every church.

Jesus' call to be a disciple is a call to apprenticeship—to submit one's life to God by becoming like our Master Teacher through the power of the Holy Spirit.

To what aim? LOVE! But let's be honest: we need someone to teach us how to do this God's way. Yes, of course, we are called to follow Jesus and not man—agreed; but we need someone to show us what following Jesus looks like. It has always been this way, even from the very beginning of the church.

Every apprentice needs a Master Teacher. Here's how to choose a good one:

1. **LOVE!** You will know by their love for God through their personal relationship with Jesus Christ.
2. **LOVE!** You will know by their love for the Word of God and how they are humbly learning to obey all that Jesus teaches through the presence and power of the Holy Spirit.
3. **LOVE!** You will know by their love for you and for people—not just church people, but the people they encounter.

Who is teaching you?

Seize the moment and "Faithfully Obey the Lord by Loving Others Well" (F.O.L.L.O.W.).

1 CORINTHIANS 5
WITH YOU IN SPIRIT!

As I write this, I miss seeing so many of the people I used to see on a regular basis a little over six months ago. As social creatures, it is a challenge to maintain the strength of community when our paths are not physically crossing in normal rhythm.

Paul knew this and wrote a lot of letters to the churches he once gathered with physically. He reached into their world even though he couldn't be physically present. He stated in 1 Corinthians 5:3, "Even though I am not physically present, I am with you in spirit" (ESV).

That was the original intent of this passion project where we reach out to the church daily with a new word from the New Testament. That is our modern-day equivalent of attempting the same thing to each of you. We desire to be together—to remain united in the Word and Spirit. We are still a community, even if our paths aren't physically crossing on a normal basis.

The circumstances of our lives have brought us at this time, and may again, to a place where unity in the Spirit is possibly more tangible than ever. If you find yourself still in that place today as you read this, send an email or card, text, letter, make a phone call—reach out to your church family and allow them to be with you in Spirit!

Seize the moment and reach out to your church family today, uniting in Spirit if you can't be physically present together.

1 CORINTHIANS 6
FREEDOM FROM BINGEING!

Have you spent any quiet time with God lately?

To binge is "to indulge in an activity … to excess." This term is popularly used for how many people do media consumption—watching countless hours of shows at a time to complete whole seasons in short order; we call this "binge-watching."

I had someone say to me recently that there are fewer than five seconds between one show ending and the next beginning. Why? Because they know that the average attention span of their younger viewing audience is that of a goldfish, which is about nine seconds. They want to grab you before something else gets your attention.

Paul addresses the entire church in a multi-chapter dialogue about church discipline and the damaging effects of sin, but the principles he gave us apply to how we personally live our lives. Listen to one of these principles from 1 Corinthians 6:12, "All things are lawful for me, but not all things are profitable. All things are lawful for me, but I will not be mastered by anything."

Paul addresses food and sex in these verses. Why is Paul dealing with such personal issues in our lives? Because God cares about our sensuality and what is competing for our attention. He cares about what we binge because, as Paul teaches us in 1 Corinthians 6:19-20, our bodies are the "temple of the Holy Spirit."

What masters your mind's thoughts, your heart's desires, and your body's neediness? I encourage you to take 15 minutes today, turn off all gadgets and sounds and just listen to where your mind goes, to what your heart feels, and what your soul yearns for. What is distracting you from focusing on God's Word and Spirit?

Seize the moment and be quiet before God. Invite God into these places. Be free from that which seeks to dominate and distract you from God.

1 CORINTHIANS 7
EXPERIENCING CONTENTMENT!

I'm writing today on my 46th birthday, and I want to thank my mom for doing all the hard work! Today, I am thanking God for the birthday gift of contentment. Contentment is very different from complacency, and they should not be confused with one another.

Contentment is defined as "the state of being mentally or emotionally satisfied."

We are called to this mental and emotional state by Jesus Christ in Matthew 6:25-33, by the Apostle Paul in Philippians 4:12-13, as well as by the author of Hebrews in Hebrews 13:5-6.

Contentment is more than an emotional or mental state; it is a way of life! 1 Corinthians 7 can be summarized with a faithful admonition from Paul to each of us in 1 Corinthians 7:17, "Only let each person lead the life that the Lord has assigned to him, and to which God has called him. This is my rule in all the churches" (ESV).

A "rule" speaks to a way of life. Paul calls Christians to a deep abiding trust in the Lord. We are to find our identity and our provision in Him and not in what we do. By contrast, humanism calls our society to a trust in ourselves and our identity—in our ability to provide for our own wants and needs. The prevailing humanistic philosophy of our culture is summarized by the saying, "He who dies with the most toys wins!" This saying gives the person who adheres to it an inability to feel secure in who they are or content in what they have.

Seize the moment and live faithfully to Jesus and the relationships He has entrusted to you. Find your identity in Him and your daily bread as from Him. Contentment is experienced when you keep your eyes on Him.

1 CORINTHIANS 8
WALK SIMPLY IN FAITH!

As a Christian, what criteria do you use to decide what to post on social media or what to say in a group setting in your church?

While we have great freedom in Christ, we should never use our freedom in such a way that it causes a brother or sister to stumble in his or her faith. Let's be direct about this: there are some conversations that should be done in-person and in a relational context, not in a large group or on a social media platform.

There is too much at stake if even one fellow believer is confused or hurt because they don't know our heart in communicating what we believe about a specific issue.

Paul explained to the early church in 1 Corinthians 8:11-12, "For through your knowledge he who is weak is ruined, the brother for whose sake Christ died. And so, by sinning against the brethren and wounding their conscience when it is weak, you sin against Christ."

I join with the Apostle Paul in exhorting the mature Christians to not let their great learning cause the simple and weak in the fellowship to stumble in what they hear and see from us—whether in person or on social media.

Seize the moment and walk simply and intentionally in your faith. Your life is for the sake of others and not for yourself! Never forget who you represent—Jesus Christ, crucified, risen, and coming again. Focus your eyes on Him and love well in His name!

1 CORINTHIANS 9
THE DISCIPLINE OF AN ATHLETE!

Christians are called to live with the discipline of an athlete.

Paul writes in 1 Corinthians 9:24-27,

Do you not know that those who run in a race all run, but only one receives the prize? Run in such a way that you may win. Everyone who competes in the games exercises self-control in all things. They then do it to receive a perishable wreath, but we an imperishable. Therefore I run in such a way, as not without aim; I box in such a way, as not beating the air; but I discipline my body and make it my slave, so that, after I have preached to others, I myself will not be disqualified.

At West Point, I was an All-American and First-Team Academic All-American in Track & Field, and then as a post-graduate I was a national team member and Olympic Team Trials finalist; I have experienced the life of an athlete at the highest amateur level.

It is not the exciting life that one would think, but a life of daily disciplines and true sacrifice. Did I love it? Honestly … Yes and No! Definitely not all the time! I had to train my whole life and exercise self-control in all things to accomplish the one goal of attaining the prize. Every part of my life, for years, was regulated by the goal—including sleep habits, eating, travel, friendships, recreation, calendar planning, time usage, and a myriad of other personal details.

The same is true in the Christian life! More so, because in the Christian life we are submitting our lives to an even greater calling than a personal goal.

In the Christian life, we are free in Christ, but we must in all things bring that freedom into submission so that our lives proclaim the good news that set us free in the first place!

Seize the moment and live in such a way that demonstrates the love that saves and the grace that transformed you from death to life.

1 CORINTHIANS 10
FREEDOM FROM PEOPLE-PLEASING!

Do you struggle with people pleasing tendencies?

Paul declares for himself, and prescribes for fellow followers of Jesus, in 1 Corinthians 10:31-33, "Whether, then, you eat or drink or whatever you do, do all to the glory of God. Give no offense either to Jews or to Greeks or to the church of God; just as I also please all men in all things, not seeking my own profit but the profit of the many, so that they may be saved."

At first glance, this teaching seems to be Paul setting an example of "people pleasing," which many of us experience as addicting on the best of days and maddening on the worst of days.

But it's not! Paul's emphasis in this verse is not on "please all men in all things" as I personally placed it for years; the emphasis is on "do all to the glory of God!" It is crucial we place accurate emphasis on Paul's teaching, just as we do with syllables in words.

Yes, we are to be pleasing to people, but it is not our life ambition to seek their approval. As followers of Jesus, we don't work for people, even when people are our work; we work for God and His purposes for our life and this world! Jesus was not people-focused in His earthly ministry. Rather, all that He did was according to God's will and for God's purposes; Jesus was God-focused even when people were in right in front of Him. Jesus was obedient and true to God which allowed Him to speak hard truths, love in the most honest of ways, and set people free from the deepest and most seductive sins within their hearts and souls.

Seize the moment and focus on glorifying God, not on pleasing people. Re-prioritize so that your life is not taken off course!

1 CORINTHIANS 11
PRIORITIZING THE LORD'S SUPPER!

What do you like most about going to the local gathering of your church family?

I hear many people talk about the music, the message, and spending time with friends and family. Occasionally, it is the partaking of the Lord's Supper with their church family.

The Lord's Supper is a central celebration of our faith walk with Jesus Christ. Paul teaches us about it in 1 Corinthians 11:23-34. Listen to the "words of institution" from verses 23-26:

> For I received from the Lord that which I also delivered to you, that the Lord Jesus in the night in which He was betrayed took bread; and when He had given thanks, He broke it and said, "This is My body, which is for you; do this in remembrance of Me." In the same way He took the cup also after supper, saying, "This cup is the new covenant in My blood; do this, as often as you drink it, in remembrance of Me." For as often as you eat this bread and drink the cup, you proclaim the Lord's death until He comes.

While there is nothing quite like doing this in community on a regular basis, there are plenty of faithful Christians who make the spiritual practice of communion a regular part of their personal rhythms of grace, either alone, with their families, or with a small group of Christian friends.

How is the Holy Spirit inviting you to prioritize the Lord's Supper as a central celebration of your faith walk with Jesus?

Seize the moment and prepare your heart for participating in the Lord's Supper. It is God's grace through Christ alone that qualifies any of us to partake of the bread and cup. You are invited!

1 CORINTHIANS 12
WE ARE BETTER TOGETHER!

I have been an athlete for most of my life. One of the hardest realities of being an athlete is staying healthy. To get to the highest levels of competition you have to push yourself to get even greater results—you can neither undertrain nor overtrain. You come to realize quickly that a significant part of success is the ability to stay healthy and prevent injury because, if even one part of the body is hurt, your whole performance decreases. It is this way in both individual and team sports; athletes depend on other people's health as much as they depend on their own health.

Paul uses the human body as an illustration to teach us about our interconnectivity and the unique importance of every member of a given congregation to the church's success in its mission. Listen to 1 Corinthians 12:12-14:

> For even as the body is one and yet has many members, and all the members of the body, though they are many, are one body, so also is Christ. For by one Spirit we were all baptized into one body, whether Jews or Greeks, whether slaves or free, and we were all made to drink of one Spirit. For the body is not one member, but many.

Paul continues to build on this imagery in verses 26-27, "And if one member suffers, all the members suffer with it; if one member is honored, all the members rejoice with it. Now you are Christ's body, and individually members of it."

Seize the moment in caring for the full body of Christ. Pay attention not only to your own spiritual vitality and relationship health, but also care for the vitality and well-being of others. The body is only as healthy as the individual members; God designed us to be better together!

1 CORINTHIANS 13
GET RIGHT WITH LOVE!

Paul teaches us about love in 1 Corinthians 13. He starts in verses 1-3 in a surprising way:

> If I speak with the tongues of men and of angels, but do not have love, I have become a noisy gong or a clanging cymbal. If I have the gift of prophecy and know all mysteries and all knowledge; and if I have all faith, so as to remove mountains, but do not have love, I am nothing. And if I give all my possessions to feed the poor, and if I surrender my body to be burned, but do not have love, it profits me nothing.

Paul starts the love chapter by taking some of the most sensational and miraculous experiences of God's activity in a person's life and reduces those gifts to being worth nothing when they are not done with the right motives of love. It's scandalous when you think about it!

Over the years, I have often said to people, "Don't be right and wrong at the same time!"

What do I mean by this? I mean the same thing Paul did: You may have a strong word of truth about a doctrine, or social issue, or perspective on culture, but if you don't conduct yourself with grace and speak that truth in love, then you are as wrong as wrong gets—no matter how right you think you are.

No amount of having the truth ever gives you permission to be unloving! At this point, the common response I get from self-righteous Christians is that Jesus turned the tables in the temple. And I say, "Yes, He did! But He didn't sin when He did it!"

Without love, you are sinning! Don't let the plank in your eye blind you to this truth.

Seize the moment and do all things in the same love with which God first loved you!

1 CORINTHIANS 14
BUILD THE FIRE OF GOD'S PRESENCE!

I enjoy a nice campfire, especially as the weather cools off; it gives off light and warmth. But the key to a good campfire on a cold autumn night is having plenty of wood to keep the fire going.

The Church is like a campfire. As the days grow darker and colder, our neighborhoods and communities need the light of Jesus and the warmth of His love. We need to add our lives to the fire to ensure it is burning hot and bright for the sake of others.

Why do you gather with your local church?

Paul focuses the eagerness of Christians with these words from 1 Corinthians 14:12, "So also you, since you are zealous of spiritual gifts, seek to abound for the edification of the church." Again, he says in verse 26, "When you assemble, each one has a psalm, has a teaching, has a revelation, has a tongue, has an interpretation. Let all things be done for edification."

These are key verses in understanding the purpose of spiritual gifts—to "edify" or build up His Church. We are to strengthen the congregation with how we participate in the public gathering of worship.

Building up the Church is our motive because the Church is the body of Christ—it is built up and held together only by love. The body of Christ requires the members live lives of love, mutually submitted to one another, completely dependent upon Jesus Christ, the Head of His Church.

Seize the moment and eagerly pursue the manifestations of the Spirit. Be sure to do so to build up the body of Christ to the glory of the One name that is above all names—the name of Jesus Christ. May His light shine brightly and the warmth of His love reach many.

1 CORINTHIANS 15
TRAIL RUNNING VS. TREADMILL RUNNING!

I am not a fan of running on the treadmill. You work awfully hard to get nowhere! My favorite place to run is out on a hiking or mountain biking trail. The scenery is beautiful, and the running is dynamic. A trail run is always rewarding, and it never feels like exercise; it is its own experience!

Paul declares in 1 Corinthians 15:58, "Therefore, my beloved brethren, be steadfast, immovable, always abounding in the work of the Lord, knowing that your toil is not in vain in the Lord."

Do you ever feel like you are running on a treadmill in work, church, or life?

To labor in vain is to work hard and get nowhere—with no apparent results or successes. As a pastor, I know that Paul gave us this verse for a very good reason! I need to know this in my heart of hearts. If you don't get this, you will burn out, or drop out, of ministry!

Here's the key—there is always a good work happening when you labor with the Lord:

1. The good seeds of the gospel are planted in people.
2. The hard ground of the human heart is softened by God's Spirit.
3. The life-giving light of God's love pierces the darkness to bring life from death.

God is always at work even if we can't see it, taking our little and making much of it! Only God can bring an increase so we must remain faithful to the process, instead of focused on the results! We are to join with Paul in his example: being steadfast, immovable, and always abounding in the work of the Lord!

We are to be faithful with what God has called us to do—with eyes on Jesus!

Seize the moment and don't get discouraged; don't bail before the blessing! When you are faithfully living in the easy yoke of Jesus, you are never running on a treadmill.

1 CORINTHIANS 16
MAKING PERSONAL CONNECTIONS!

As Paul concludes this letter, he personally comments in 1 Corinthians 16:15-18,

> Now I urge you, brethren (you know the household of Stephanas, that they were the first fruits of Achaia, and that they have devoted themselves for ministry to the saints), that you also be in subjection to such men and to everyone who helps in the work and labors. I rejoice over the coming of Stephanas and Fortunatus and Achaicus, because they have supplied what was lacking on your part. For they have refreshed my spirit and yours. Therefore acknowledge such men.

The last chapter of Corinthians is filled with personal remarks, greetings, and preparations for travels. I find great joy in seeing personal remarks in the Bible, travel plans, everyday communications that people who love one another would make as they stay in touch.

Paul says of the people in the Corinthian church, "they have refreshed my spirit and yours" (18). Who refreshes your spirit in your church? Do you look forward to seeing the people with whom you worship each week? Whose spirit are you refreshing?

Today, we can do this through numerous social media platforms, e-mails, texts, phones, and the classic hand-written letter or card. But nothing replaces being face-to-face with someone, refreshing one another by being together. I am convinced of the importance of making personal relationships in small groups, during Sunday School classes, through just hanging out with one another, and by worshipping together on the Lord's Day. We are called to love one another and to make space in our lives to know and be known.

Seize the moment and reach out today to make a personal connection with someone. Make a commitment to return to the public gathering of worship, or your small group or Sunday School class. Then, invite someone to join you. Encourage another person. You never know how a personal invitation could bless someone. Don't wait for someone else, you make the call today.

2 CORINTHIANS 1
SEALED FOR DELIVERY!

Have you ever trusted a carrier service with anything of great value? Did you worry about it getting to its location and then give a sigh of relief when it arrived on time as guaranteed? Did you go so far as requiring a signature-upon-delivery guarantee to ensure it got to the right person?

With those questions in mind, read what Paul says in 2 Corinthians 1:20-22, "For as many as are the promises of God, in Him they are yes; therefore also through Him is our Amen to the glory of God through us. Now He who establishes us with you in Christ and anointed us is God, who also sealed us and gave us the Spirit in our hearts as a pledge."

Jesus Christ, the Son of God and Savior of the World, defeated death and atoned for sin. Though we deserve death, deserve the penalty for sin, and deserve the full outpouring of God's wrath, Jesus Christ took those willingly, lovingly, and fully upon Himself so that we, God's prodigal children, may come home to Him without penalty. In fact, we now receive the fullness of blessing from God because of Christ's victory. This fullness is the outpouring of the Holy Spirit upon us, which Paul calls the "seal."

In ancient days, kings would authenticate messages with a unique seal that was their mark. It was a guarantee of authenticity as well as a security for delivery. The seal set it apart as the king's property.

Your salvation—signed and sealed—is guaranteed to be delivered to the right location at the right time! You don't need to fret about or worry about it! The King of kings' seal is upon you!

Seize the moment and rest in the seal of the Holy Spirit. Walk in the power, presence, and peace of the God who dwells in you!

2 CORINTHIANS 2
THE ART OF FORGIVENESS!

It was said to me in a very tender situation that "forgiveness is the heart of Christianity." I was at a very low moment in my life and, honestly, I was bracing myself to be taken even lower when this person said this to me. Through Christ's shed blood on the Cross, this person's forgiveness released me. I will never forget, and I praise God!

As you read 2 Corinthians 2, you will hear Paul writing about a very difficult situation in the church that brought much heartache and pain. Through this incident we learn about the awkward work of mutual accountability, and the harder work of forgiveness. It is never one without the other—there is always a need for both. Church discipline is a call to both reconciliation and restoration!

Paul explains in 2 Corinthians 2:10-11, "But one whom you forgive anything, I forgive also; for indeed what I have forgiven, if I have forgiven anything, I did it for your sakes in the presence of Christ, so that no advantage would be taken of us by Satan, for we are not ignorant of his schemes."

Is there someone you need to talk to today? Do you feel that you are justified to ignore or hang on to the offense? Do you think it's their responsibility and not your own? The initiative is in your hands to reach out and reconcile and restore your relationships.

Praise God Jesus didn't think that way; He didn't wait for us to come to Him before He came to us! You and I are forgiven because that is the work of the Cross, for undeserving people like you and me, and for whoever this other person is. Forgiveness is the heart of Christianity!

Seize the moment and forgive today! It will set you free; withholding forgiveness binds you in the schemes of Satan. Get out of your prison today—forgive!

2 CORINTHIANS 3
SACRED BEAUTY IN ORDINARY LIVES!

We are created and rescued to be restored Image Bearers of God's presence in His creation—we are called by God to reflect His image to the world by how we love, care for, and steward His creation. This world is our home and, as God promises in Revelation 21 and 22, it is His future eternal Home—the New Heaven and New Earth.

That means there is a sacred beauty to our ordinary lives! We are to reflect the glory of God as with unveiled faces. Our lives point to who and what is coming!

Paul teaches us this powerful truth in 1 Corinthians 3:17-18, "Now the Lord is the Spirit, and where the Spirit of the Lord is, there is liberty. But we all, with unveiled face, beholding as in a mirror the glory of the Lord, are being transformed into the same image from glory to glory, just as from the Lord, the Spirit."

The more time we spend with God, the more we will reflect His glory and grace to others. The more familiar we are with His Word, the more our words will reflect His glory and truth to others. Our stories will point to Jesus Christ, crucified, risen, and coming again.

Like the moon, we have no glory of our own. We, too, are designed by the Creator to reflect the Light of the Son. May your life be so free in the Spirit that you reflect the glory of God more and more in your daily life—may there be a sacred beauty in your ordinary comings and goings.

Seize the moment and shine His light and love by how you love, care for, and steward God's creation around you.

2 CORINTHIANS 4
A BILLBOARD OF GOD'S GLORY!

Your life is a billboard in lights!

Listen to 2 Corinthians 4:6-7,

For God, who said, "Light shall shine out of darkness," is the One who has shone in our hearts to give the Light of the knowledge of the glory of God in the face of Christ. But we have this treasure in earthen vessels ["jars of clay" in the ESV], so that the surpassing greatness of the power will be of God and not from ourselves.

God's presence changes you and, by design, the mystery of God is made known through you because the Holy Spirit now dwells in you. God has redeemed your life for an even greater purpose—to put something on display other than yourself. What a mystery and what grace!

This is the most liberating truth in the world, a balm to my soul. If I was the point of the story and my perfection was the point of the story, then what bondage I would experience as a Christian. But I am not the point; it is the treasure that has been placed in me that is the point!

The pressure is not on me to polish the outside of the vessel (to whitewash and cover it up), but to show the surpassing power that belongs to God and has been placed in my life by His grace and for His glory! Simply: I am a billboard of God's glory!

It's a humbling thought, but maybe God chose you and I so that other people would see us and think to themselves—if God could save a wretch like that, then He can love me too.

Seize the moment and shine the glory of God that has been given to you! God's precious gift has not been given to be hoarded as your private ticket to heaven, but rather heralded as God's billboard of His presence in the world.

2 CORINTHIANS 5
A NEW DAY!

It's a new day with new opportunities! What is your mindset when you start a new day?

Paul teaches us in 2 Corinthians 5:6-9,

Therefore, being always of good courage, and knowing that while we are at home in the body we are absent from the Lord—for we walk by faith, not by sight—we are of good courage, I say, and prefer rather to be absent from the body and to be at home with the Lord. Therefore we also have as our ambition, whether at home or absent, to be pleasing to Him.

The faith we are given, and called into, is a deep trust of who God is, the assurance of what He has already done, and the hope of what He will complete, so that we may confidently live by grace in obedience to His commandments, fulfilling the purposes for our lives.

Faith fills us with courage regardless of what appears to be on the horizon in a new day. Faith gives us the courage to do more than survive another day; it allows us to thrive for God's glory—to hope for the New Heaven and New Earth and to live accordingly.

Our faith reminds us that we know the One who calls forth every sunrise as a gift—your life is pure grace!

Lamentations 3:22-24 teaches us, "The LORD'S lovingkindnesses indeed never cease, For His compassions never fail. They are new every morning; Great is Your faithfulness. 'The LORD is my portion,' says my soul, 'Therefore I have hope in Him.'"

Nothing on the horizon of this new day is a surprise to God. Be of good courage; live by faith and not by sight! Put your trust and hope in Jesus today!

Seize the moment and make it your aim to be of good courage and please God today!

2 CORINTHIANS 6
EVERY CRISIS IS AN OPPORTUNITY!

Every crisis is an opportunity! Do you believe that? How are you responding to your circumstances?

Paul writes in 2 Corinthians 6:3-10,

Giving no cause for offense in anything, so that the ministry will not be discredited, but in everything commending ourselves as servants of God, in much endurance, in afflictions, in hardships, in distresses, in beatings, in imprisonments, in tumults, in labors, in sleeplessness, in hunger, in purity, in knowledge, in patience, in kindness, in the Holy Spirit, in genuine love, in the word of truth, in the power of God; by the weapons of righteousness for the right hand and the left, by glory and dishonor, by evil report and good report; regarded as deceivers and yet true; as unknown yet well-known, as dying yet behold, we live; as punished yet not put to death, as sorrowful yet always rejoicing, as poor yet making many rich, as having nothing yet possessing all things.

Are you willing to allow all things in your life to point to God's grace?

It should not surprise us that hardship, persecution, and suffering are a part of the Christian life. Even a cursory reading of Jesus' words, and the rest of the New Testament, will testify to this reality. Contemporary teachings have minimized this reality, but that does not help the cause of Christ—rather, it weakens the Church.

The world is watching us and how we respond to the curve balls that are thrown at us as the people of God!

Remember, it is not our circumstances that testify to the grace of God; it is how we walk through those circumstances that testifies to the presence of God in us!

Seize the moment and use your circumstances for God's glory! Remember, every crisis is an opportunity!

2 CORINTHIANS 7
GODLY GRIEF!

Did you know that grief is an important reality of our human experience?

Listen to Paul in 2 Corinthians 7:8-10 (ESV),

For even if I made you grieve with my letter, I do not regret it—though I did regret it, for I see that that letter grieved you, though only for a while. As it is, I rejoice, not because you were grieved, but because you were grieved into repenting. For you felt a godly grief, so that you suffered no loss through us. For godly grief produces a repentance that leads to salvation without regret, whereas worldly grief produces death.

In this passage, Paul distinguishes between Godly and worldly grief.

How we deal with the events of our lives that cause grief is an essential part of our Christian discipleship. While each person will grieve in a personal way, and we must make allowances for that, there are biblical principles to follow so that we don't find our way into despair caused by worldly grief which, as Paul teaches, "produces death."

To avoid worldly grief, we are invited to respond to Godly grief with the 3 Rs:

1. **Remember Hope!** In Christ, we do not grieve as the world grieves; we grieve with hope (1 Thessalonians 4:13).
2. **Repent For Your Life's Sake!** Godly grief is real; the sorrow of the situation is real! Don't deny Godly grief; it requires a response. Respond to your grief and sorrow by allowing God to do deep surgery in your soul.
3. **Restore Right Relationships!** Keep short accounts with God and people. Value healthy relationships.

Seize the moment and be a hope-bearer, not a doomsdayer! We all will grieve, but let us grieve according to our birthright, with faith, hope, and love!

2 CORINTHIANS 8
THE GRACE OF GIVING!

Did you know that a generous lifestyle brings glory to God?

Listen to Paul's motives for giving in 2 Corinthians 8:9, "For you know the grace of our Lord Jesus Christ, that though He was rich, yet for your sake He became poor, so that you through His poverty might become rich."

Generosity gives glory to God because that is who our God is—we serve a generous God! Just look at Jesus, who made us rich through His glorious generosity. This is the gift of salvation made possible only through the life, death, and resurrection of Jesus Christ!

This is the extravagant love of John 3:16!

Our giving is worship to who God is. Our giving is the celebration of what Jesus Christ gave to us. Our giving is freedom from our insecurity and self-centered lifestyles. Our giving is glorious generosity for all to see and witness to what Christ first did for us—the transformation of our story through the glorious gospel!

Paul says in 2 Corinthians 8:7, "But just as you abound in everything, in faith and utterance and knowledge and in all earnestness and in the love we inspired in you, see that you abound in this gracious work also."

Seize the moment and practically point people to the glory of God by excelling in the grace of giving! Remember: what you do with your money reflects the god you truly serve!

2 CORINTHIANS 9
GOD'S BOUNTIFUL PROMISE!

It is always interesting to me when people share with me that they don't find the Bible practical in their everyday lives. If you find yourself thinking the same way, check out 2 Corinthians 9. Maybe the deeper issue is that the Bible pokes its nose into the intimate places of our lives, like how we deal with money.

Money matters because how we spend money shows what we value!

I encourage you to read 2 Corinthians 9, especially verses 6-15. You will find some beautiful teaching and powerful promises that have the potential to liberate you from fear and insecurity, as well as elevate your worship to a God who loves you in ways that words cannot fully express!

Paul promises us in 2 Corinthians 9:6, "He who sows sparingly will also reap sparingly, and he who sows bountifully will also reap bountifully."

It is my heart's desire that you will decide today to sow bountifully so that God can reap a bountiful harvest in your life. I am not preaching a prosperity gospel to you; I am simply asking you to trust God at His word, especially in the areas of your insecurities and fears, such as with your money.

Can you take God at His Word? As Malachi 3:10 promises, "'Bring the whole tithe into the storehouse, so that there may be food in My house, and test Me now in this,' says the LORD of hosts, 'if I will not open for you the windows of heaven and pour out for you a blessing until it overflows.'"

There is only one way to know if you can trust God and His promises. It is through belief that you will experience the bountiful promises of God!

Seize the moment and trust God today by living a generous lifestyle.

2 CORINTHIANS 10
DAILY VICTORIES!

Are you winning the daily victories in your Christian life?

Paul says in 2 Corinthians 10:4-6,

For the weapons of our warfare are not of the flesh, but divinely powerful for the destruction of fortresses. We are destroying speculations and every lofty thing raised up against the knowledge of God, and we are taking every thought captive to the obedience of Christ, and we are ready to punish all disobedience, whenever your obedience is complete.

A fortress is a military term that gives us the image of an enemy stronghold that has been established in your rightful homeland that causes you to live a limited life; a life other than the abundant life Jesus promised in John 10:10.

In everyday ways, a stronghold is like a kink in a garden hose—a garden hose is intended to bring fresh drinkable water from the source to the destination, but the stronghold blocks the flow of God's Spirit through you so that you do not manifest the fruit of the Spirit or utilize the gifts of the Spirit for the work God has called you to do.

In the context, Paul is specifically talking about strongholds of thoughts and ideas, and the accompanying behaviors that flow from an unbiblical belief system.

One of the ways I am winning daily victories is by writing daily devotions through the COVID-19 pandemic. These help me fight the good fight for Christ; my devotional time is a pathway of relationship with God, and I hope it is the beginning point for you to make time for God in each of your days.

We each must destroy strongholds, and take every thought captive, so that we may walk in obedience to the commandments of Jesus Christ and bring God glory through our everyday decisions.

Seize the moment and structure your life for daily victories. Spend time in God's Word today.

2 CORINTHIANS 11
PRAY FOR YOUR CHURCH!

How is your prayer life for your local church and the larger Church throughout the nation and world?

Paul makes a big statement that can easily be missed in his long list of sufferings for Christ. He writes in 2 Corinthians 11:28, "Apart from such external things, there is the daily pressure on me of concern for all the churches."

The "external things" Paul referenced is found in verses 21-33, and actually continues into chapter 12. Paul clearly went through a lot to be faithful to God's call upon his life as an Apostle of Jesus Christ to the Gentiles. He suffered greatly, and in many ways, but Paul is highlighting something here that we can relate to.

Paul says that he feels a daily pressure of concern for the churches.

Are you concerned for the state of the American Church, or for the persecuted Church throughout the world, or for the unity of the Church in its many denominations and variations? Maybe you have a more specific local concern for one specific church, or locality of churches. Even more specifically, maybe you have a concern for a specific person, or group of people, in a church or community.

However you are experiencing the daily pressure of concern for the Church, it is my hope that you will bring that concern to the Lord in prayer. Are you praying for the Church and its leaders?

Seize the moment and make time to pray for your church and the larger Church. As Paul teaches us in 1 Thessalonians 5:16-18, "Rejoice always; pray without ceasing; in everything give thanks; for this is God's will for you in Christ Jesus."

2 CORINTHIANS 12
SELF-SUFFICIENCY VS. GOD'S SUFFICIENCY!

I don't like failing! I prefer to be sufficient to accomplish whatever task that needs to be done, but that whole mindset is a dangerous trap of pride and arrogance.

There is no rest in self-sufficiency!

Paul shares an important word from the Lord in 2 Corinthians 12:9-10:

And [the Lord] has said to me, "My grace is sufficient for you, for power is perfected in weakness." Most gladly, therefore, I will rather boast about my weaknesses, so that the power of Christ may dwell in me. Therefore, I am well content with weaknesses, with insults, with distresses, with persecutions, with difficulties, for Christ's sake; for when I am weak, then I am strong.

The teachings of Jesus Christ are counter-intuitive to our corrupted desires for self-sufficiency and power. We want to live as independent, powerful beings, but God has hard-wired us to be dependent creatures—dependent on God and on one another!

My weaknesses constantly remind me of my inability to live this life on my own power. For it is only then, when I am confronted with my weaknesses, that I can begin to live according to God's design, in harmony with why Jesus came to show us the way and to die for our true freedom.

Christ emptied Himself so that we can be become full of Him! We are freed from self-sufficiency to live in God's sufficiency!

Seize the moment and find rest, not in the ongoing work of your own hands, but in the finished work of His nail-scarred hands. Not from the sweat on your own brow, but in the shed blood of His thorn-pierced brow. Surrender to God's sufficiency today!

2 CORINTHIANS 13
PASSING THE TEST!

Recently, I completed my doctorate. It was a wonderful four years, and my fourth college degree. I love school! Do you? Do you remember taking tests in school?

Honestly, everyone gets a little nervous when they hear the word test, even life-long students like me, so what should we do when Paul says in 2 Corinthians 13:5, "Examine yourselves to see whether you are in the faith; test yourselves"?

What should such a test look like?

Let's get some context for his statement: Paul lays out his goal in 2 Corinthians 13:9-11, stating,

> For we rejoice when we ourselves are weak but you are strong; this we also pray for, that you be made complete. For this reason I am writing these things while absent, so that when present I need not use severity, in accordance with the authority which the Lord gave me for building up and not for tearing down. Finally, brethren, rejoice, be made complete, be comforted, be like-minded, live in peace; and the God of love and peace will be with you.

Based on this, there would be 4 questions to determine whether or not you would pass the test he calls us to:

1. Are you rejoicing in the presence of the God of love and peace?

2. Are your relationships "complete," meaning they are spiritually healthy and filled with wholeness, forgiveness, and grace?

3. Are you comforting one another in the hardships, griefs, and loneliness of life?

4. Are you living in peace with yourself and others throughout all circumstances?

Seize the moment and examine yourself today. By yourself, under your own power, it is impossible to pass this test, but with God all things are possible.

GALATIANS, EPHESIANS, PHILIPPIANS, AND COLOSSIANS

GALATIANS 1
YOU CAN'T SERVE TWO MASTERS!

Paul emphasizes from the very beginning of his letter to the Christians in the region of Galatia that the Gospel he received and proclaimed is not from man; it is from Jesus Christ. Paul's ministry as an apostle to the Gentiles (non-Jewish people) is a grace bestowed upon him by God. Neither his faith nor his ministry is of himself; it is all from God. Therefore, he lives and does everything for God. Paul was very clear about whom he served, and it was not the Church or any man, including himself and his good intentions.

His ministry would not have been as effective or impactful over the past two thousand years if it was man he was serving. When we serve God, God can use us in ways that are beyond our imaginations.

Listen to Paul from Galatians 1:10, "For am I now seeking the favor of man, or of God? Or am I trying to please men? If I were still trying to please men, I would not be a bond-servant of Christ."

Paul breaks people-pleasing down to a simple choice: you serve man, or you serve Christ! This is one of those either/or moments that confronts us. Refusing to acknowledge the choice put before each of us this day and stubbornly believing that we can serve both God and man ensures we become entrenched in people-pleasing patterns of living. Humbling ourselves and acknowledging the Holy Spirit's confrontation of our motives and intentions sets our face and feet to seeking first the Kingdom of God and His righteousness, trusting that all these other things will be added unto us (Jesus' words from Matthew 6:33).

So, today, I ask: Who do you serve?

Seize the moment and seek first the Kingdom of God and His righteousness.

GALATIANS 2
ON PURPOSE CHRISTIANS!

Paul explains about our salvation in Galatians 2:16 and 20,

Knowing that a man is not justified by the works of the Law but through faith in Christ Jesus, even we have believed in Christ Jesus, so that we may be justified by faith in Christ and not by the works of the Law; since by the works of the Law no flesh will be justified. … I have been crucified with Christ; and it is no longer I who live, but Christ lives in me; and the life which I now live in the flesh I live by faith in the Son of God, who loved me and gave Himself up for me.

Jesus Christ gave His life for a purpose—so that God's family can be restored to Him. That means you can be saved—accepted, justified, redeemed, restored into right relationship with God through the shed blood of Jesus Christ. Jesus lived and died on purpose!

All of us who claim Christ as Lord and Savior are called to live with the same intentional focus, on purpose, for Jesus Christ. This intentional focus doesn't begin and end with receiving Christ through faith; we are also called to live our lives on purpose for Jesus, reflecting thankfulness for His life, death, and resurrection.

Many understand and embrace their salvation, and many celebrate it every Sunday! However, do each of us understand that we are called, saved, and transformed by the love of God to walk with Jesus, and His purposes, to restore God's family back to Him?

Seize the moment and live on purpose for Jesus!

GALATIANS 3
ABSOLUTE DEPENDENCE!

We all have favorite passages of the Bible. One of my favorites is Galatians 3:3 because of its deep impact upon my testimony as a pastor who is learning to be totally dependent on the Word and Spirit instead of dependent on my own competencies and charisma.

Listen to Paul's questions in Galatians 3:3, "Are you so foolish? Having begun by the Spirit, are you now being perfected by the flesh?"

I was on a silent retreat in 2015 when this Scripture came alive and spoke personally to me. The Lord was graciously teaching me, and is still teaching me, absolute dependence on Him—a full surrender, a forsaking of all, a crucified life. This was the beginning of the journey that has led me to learn the life of a Yokefellow—the life of the easy yoke of Jesus Christ (Matthew 11:28-30).

When we learn to work from grace and work restfully, then we can do much for God without hurry in our souls because our souls are at rest in Him. We learn that all things, from justification to glorification, to every step of sanctification along the way, come only from grace and not from anything we can do!

When we learn to stop being foolish and stop trying to work under our own power to do what only God can do through His Holy Spirit, then we stop fighting against God's will for our lives. Seeking and obeying God's will for our lives is sanctification, which is our conformity to the image of Christ, for the glory of the Father, through the indwelling of the Holy Spirit.

Seize the moment and learn to submit to the work of the Holy Spirit in you. Total dependence on Him is the life of faith.

GALATIANS 4
LIVE THE REAL DEAL!

Do you know how bankers learn the difference between real money and counterfeit bills?

They study the real thing so that they know what is right and true.

In the same way, Paul calls us not to live according to the "elemental things of the world," but according to the Word of God. Listen to Galatians 4:3-7:

> So also we, while we were children, were held in bondage under the elemental things of the world. But when the fullness of the time came, God sent forth His Son, born of a woman, born under the Law, so that He might redeem those who were under the Law, that we might receive the adoption as sons. Because you are sons, God has sent forth the Spirit of His Son into our hearts, crying, "Abba! Father!" Therefore you are no longer a slave, but a son; and if a son, then an heir through God.

Examine these three contrasts between the counterfeit and the real:

1. The world calls you to be a consumer for treasures, the Spirit of God calls you to be a container for the glorious treasure of Christ in you. You are saved to shine His marvelous light!
2. The world calls you to hoard so that you can feel security in your possessions, the Spirit calls you to give generously of what you have so that you can find your security in the One who possesses you. You are not owned by your possessions!
3. The world calls you to live a happy life by indulging your desires and living according to their dictates, the Spirit calls you to a joyful life by crucifying your flesh and its desires so that you are not imprisoned to them. You are free in Christ!

Seize the moment and live for the real deal—you are not a slave to fear, you are a child of God!

GALATIANS 5
TRUE FREEDOM!

What does the Bible say about our freedom?

Paul explains in Galatians 5:1, "It was for freedom that Christ set us free; therefore keep standing firm and do not be subject again to a yoke of slavery."

From what has Christ set us free? In one word: sin. Sin is rebellion against God and His revealed will for our lives. The Bible teaches us that we all have gone our own way and done what it is right in our own eyes and that prevents us from being members of His household (Romans 3:23). You see, sin separates us from God and from the true freedom He has for us.

Sin breaks relationships! That's the bad news, but what is the good news?

When we confess our sin and turn away from its control of our lives by surrendering to Jesus Christ as our Lord and Savior, we receive eternal life and are set free from sin; we are now forgiven to live a new way—"the new way of the Spirit" (Romans 7:6)—in a renewed relationship with God!

In Galatians 5:13-14, Paul says it this way, "For you were called to freedom, brethren; only do not turn your freedom into an opportunity for the flesh, but through love serve one another. For the whole law is fulfilled in one word, in the statement, 'You shall love your neighbor as yourself.'"

Love! Love is the evidence of your freedom! The test of your freedom is how you walk in the Spirit, which is most clearly made visible in how you think about and treat other people.

True freedom is the freedom to live and love in healthy relationships—first with God, and then with others.

Seize the moment and walk in true freedom—Love God and love people!

GALATIANS 6
THE RIGHT TIME FOR RIGHT RELATIONSHIPS!

Have you ever had a hard time with relationships?

Paul exhorts us in Galatians 6:1-2, "Brethren, even if anyone is caught in any trespass, you who are spiritual, restore such a one in a spirit of gentleness; each one looking to yourself, so that you too will not be tempted. Bear one another's burdens, and thereby fulfill the law of Christ."

Let me highlight three simple principles to help us have right relationships:

1. "Anyone" means every person and "any trespass" means any and all offenses of which you can think or imagine. We need to make a premeditated decision to forgive and grant grace to people.

2. We are called to restore the person "in a spirit of gentleness." Gentleness is a Fruit of the Spirit (Galatians 5:22-23), which means if you feel like you can't do this all the time every time, you are right! God invites you to submit to His Spirit and let Him love people through you! As Christians, we don't represent ourselves or our self-interest; we represent Jesus and the Kingdom of God.

3. Focus on being healthy. I truly believe many people are walking around looking like they have it all together, but, in the moment, they have the emotional intelligence of a teenager. Paul says, "Each one looking to yourself, so that you too will not be tempted." We are called to be emotionally and spiritually intelligent enough to rise above the hot mess of our circumstances to be different. We are not to give ourselves over to the offenses and irresponsible behaviors of the people around us.

No matter what is happening, right now—amid whatever circumstances we face—is the right time to focus on right relationships!

Seize the moment and remain faithful to God and others.

EPHESIANS 1
THANKFUL TO BE BLESSED!

I've noticed that more and more people are using the word "Blessed!" to describe themselves, their families, and their situations.

Listen to how Paul starts off his letter in Ephesians 1:3, "Blessed be the God and Father of our Lord Jesus Christ, who has blessed us in Christ with every spiritual blessing in the heavenly places."

In the NIV, the first "blessed" is translated "Praise" as in "Praise be to the God and Father …" That should tell us something right away about this rich word.

It is true and right for a Christian to say they are blessed; in Christ we have every spiritual blessing in the heavenly places. This is an amazing truth of God's Word, and one of the promises of God to us! Praise be to God who has done this and given this gift to us!

What does it mean to be blessed? It means that we are forgiven and adopted by the Father, redeemed through the shed blood of Jesus Christ, and sealed by the indwelling of the Holy Spirit. Please keep reading Ephesians 1:3-14 to learn more.

Jesus Christ has blessed us, and brought us to God, by taking all the curses of God that we deserve for our sin onto Himself and has given us His relationship with God—His righteousness (2 Corinthians 5:21). In Christ, God will never withhold any blessing from you because you rightfully and legally belong to Him as an adopted son with right of inheritance as one of His chosen people.

That is a Good Father. This is your heavenly blessing as a child of God!

Seize the moment and be thankful—you have been blessed to be a blessing!

EPHESIANS 2
THE GIFT OF HOPE!

We all need faith, hope, and love in our darkest days, so let us turn to God's Word for the living hope—Jesus Christ.

Paul writes in Ephesians 2:4-9,

But God, being rich in mercy, because of His great love with which He loved us, even when we were dead in our transgressions, made us alive together with Christ (by grace you have been saved), and raised us up with Him, and seated us with Him in the heavenly places in Christ Jesus, so that in the ages to come He might show the surpassing riches of His grace in kindness toward us in Christ Jesus. For by grace you have been saved through faith; and that not of yourselves, it is the gift of God; not as a result of works, so that no one may boast.

The only hope that will never disappoint us is our hope in the love God gives to us through faith in Jesus Christ.

"But God ..." Those two words in Scripture change everything. Never forget those two words, no matter how difficult your trials and tribulations, "but God."

Death – but God!
Disease – but God!
Depression – but God!
Disappointment – but God!
COVID-19 – but God!

Seize the moment and rest in the promises of God for your life and the lives of your loved ones. Whatever giant you may be facing today, remember, "but God ..." This is the gift of hope!

EPHESIANS 3
PRAYING BIG PRAYERS!

Paul prays big prayers for the congregation in Ephesus in Ephesians 3:14-21:

> For this reason I bow my knees before the Father, from whom every family in heaven and on earth derives its name, that He would grant you, according to the riches of His glory, to be strengthened with power through His Spirit in the inner man, so that Christ may dwell in your hearts through faith; and that you, being rooted and grounded in love, may be able to comprehend with all the saints what is the breadth and length and height and depth, and to know the love of Christ which surpasses knowledge, that you may be filled up to all the fullness of God. Now to Him who is able to do far more abundantly beyond all that we ask or think, according to the power that works within us, to Him be the glory in the church and in Christ Jesus to all generations forever and ever. Amen.

Through Jesus Christ's sacrificial death on the Cross of Calvary we are invited—commanded—to approach the throne of grace boldly, with confidence. We are to pray big prayers according to the revelation of our God we have been given.

I have heard many people say they don't pray big prayers because they think God has more important things to which He must attend. That kind of attitude shows our lack of understanding of God's perfection and immensity, and that is why Paul prays for you to know how BIG God is intimately and thoroughly. Paul prays for you to be filled with all the fullness of God. These are big prayers; are you praying big prayers for your family, church, community, and world?

Seize the moment and pray God's Word today. Pray the promises of God.

EPHESIANS 4
WALK IN A MANNER WORTHY!

Are you walking in a manner worthy of the calling of Jesus Christ?

Paul says in Ephesians 4:1-3 (ESV), "I therefore, a prisoner for the Lord, urge you to walk in a manner worthy of the calling to which you have been called, with all humility and gentleness, with patience, bearing with one another in love, eager to maintain the unity of the Spirit in the bond of peace."

The Koine Greek word translated "worthy" means "fitting or proper in corresponding to what should be expected—proper, properly, fitting, worthy of, correspond to." So, when Paul exhorts us to walk in a manner worthy of the calling, he is essentially saying: ensure your life corresponds with the gospel of Jesus Christ.

Do you live like someone who has been saved? When people see you, do they think of God's grace? Do they see Jesus?

Speaking of grace, a major emphasis of Paul's writing is that we can't do this on our own power, but only under the authority, or power, of the Holy Spirit. From Ephesians 4:1-3, Paul gives some criteria to know whether you are walking in a manner worthy of the new life we have been given by God's grace through Jesus Christ:

1.   Humility.
2.   Gentleness.
3.   Patience.
4.   Bearing with one another in love.
5.   Eager to maintain unity of the Spirit.
6.   Eager to maintain the bond of peace.

Interestingly, there are some intersections between these criteria and Paul's writing on the Fruit of the Spirit in Galatians 5:22-23.

So, how are you doing in your walk? Does your life demonstrate Monday-Saturday what you proclaim when you gather as His Church on Sundays? Our day-to-day life is our faith and our witness.

Seize the moment and walk in a manner worthy of your calling.

EPHESIANS 5
BE A WAKE-UP CALL!

Have you ever been asleep when someone turns on the light in the room? It definitely wakes you up!

Paul teaches us in Ephesians 5:8-14,

For you were formerly darkness, but now you are Light in the Lord; walk as children of Light (for the fruit of the Light consists in all goodness and righteousness and truth), trying to learn what is pleasing to the Lord. Do not participate in the unfruitful deeds of darkness, but instead even expose them; for it is disgraceful even to speak of the things which are done by them in secret. But all things become visible when they are exposed by the light, for everything that becomes visible is light. For this reason it says, "Awake, sleeper, and arise from the dead, and Christ will shine on you."

Darkness is a lack of the true substance—light! Before Christ, we all were in darkness. The Bible teaches us that before Jesus we were cut off from God—literally "dead in [our] transgressions." In Jesus, we are the light of the world because we are now "alive with Christ" (Ephesians 2:4-5).

Jesus loves us so much that He would take our death (our darkness) for us so that we can share in His life (His light)—we are now the light to the world only because He is the light of the world (Matthew 5:14-16)! He is alive in us. We have gone from death to life!

Just like when the light is turned on in that dark room and you go from being asleep to suddenly awake, Christians are saved to be a wake-up call to the world, proclaiming, "Awake, sleeper, and arise from the dead, and Christ will shine on you."

Seize the moment and be a wake-up call to all you encounter! Shine!

EPHESIANS 6
THE GREATEST WEAPON!

Paul teaches us in Ephesians 6:18, "With all prayer and petition pray at all times in the Spirit, and with this in view, be on the alert with all perseverance and petition for all the saints."

What a beautiful passage! It is a partner passage to Philippians 4:6-7, "Be anxious for nothing, but in everything by prayer and supplication with thanksgiving let your requests be made known to God. And the peace of God, which surpasses all comprehension, will guard your hearts and your minds in Christ Jesus."

Both of these Scriptures exhort us to use prayer as an offensive, proactive weapon in the power of the Spirit of God. We have been equipped to face any giant because we remember that the battle belongs to the Lord. We simply get to be witnesses to His faithfulness!

It's also important to note that the context of Ephesians 6:18 is putting on the full armor of God. How do we join with God in this battle for the hearts and minds of individuals, families, communities, and nations?

We have to make sure we are only using the weapons of the Spirit so that we can stand firm on the rock of Jesus Christ:

1.   Praying in the Spirit on all occasions.
2.   Making petitions and requests in everything.
3.   Giving thanks to God in all of our prayers, petitions, and requests.

Let me summarize these in one statement: **The proactive prayers and petitions of thanksgiving are our greatest weapon!**

We so often forget that thankfulness is not a reactive emotional response to our circumstances, but, rather, a proactive awareness of God's faithfulness in everything.

Seize the moment and pray in the Spirit on all occasions through the proactive prayers and petitions of thanksgiving! Your thanksgiving is your continual praise to God!

PHILIPPIANS 1
WALKING IN THE PROMISES OF GOD!

Paul leads with a promise from God in Philippians 1:6: "For I am confident of this very thing, that He who began a good work in you will perfect it until the day of Christ Jesus."

Paul moves to prayer in verses 9-11:

And this I pray, that your love may abound still more and more in real knowledge and all discernment, so that you may approve the things that are excellent, in order to be sincere and blameless until the day of Christ; having been filled with the fruit of righteousness which comes through Jesus Christ, to the glory and praise of God.

Paul then gives us some perspective in verse 12: "Now I want you to know, brethren, that my circumstances have turned out for the greater progress of the gospel."

Paul finally gives us the plan in verse 21: "For to me, to live is Christ and to die is gain."

In life, all four of the following elements are important to live the victorious life in Christ:

1. Promise to claim.
2. Prayer to pray.
3. Proper perspective on circumstances.
4. Plan to walk.

Without any one of these four elements you may find yourself overwhelmed by an anxious mind or fearful heart, aimless in your life, and buried in your circumstances. It is my desire to help you choose the better way—the way of the Spirit, which is the crucified life in Christ.

Seize the moment and walk in the promises of God. When we live by the promises of God, we truly walk in union with Jesus Christ and experience God's best for our lives.

PHILIPPIANS 2
WALK LIKE JESUS WALKED!

Paul recorded the Christ Hymn of the New Testament Church in Philippians 2:5-11:

> Have this attitude in yourselves which was also in Christ Jesus, who, although He existed in the form of God, did not regard equality with God a thing to be grasped, but emptied Himself, taking the form of a bond-servant, and being made in the likeness of men. Being found in appearance as a man, He humbled Himself by becoming obedient to the point of death, even death on a cross. For this reason also, God highly exalted Him, and bestowed on Him the name which is above every name, so that at the name of Jesus every knee will bow, of those who are in heaven and on earth and under the earth, and that every tongue will confess that Jesus Christ is Lord, to the glory of God the Father.

Based upon Jesus' example of self-emptying, Paul calls maturing Christians to a life of humility and love in Philippians 2:14-18:

> Do all things without grumbling or disputing; so that you will prove yourselves to be blameless and innocent, children of God above reproach in the midst of a crooked and perverse generation, among whom you appear as lights in the world, holding fast the word of life, so that in the day of Christ I will have reason to glory because I did not run in vain nor toil in vain. But even if I am being poured out as a drink offering upon the sacrifice and service of your faith, I rejoice and share my joy with you all. You too, I urge you, rejoice in the same way and share your joy with me.

Seize the moment and ask the Holy Spirit to help you walk faithfully with Jesus today by:

* Doing all things without grumbling or disputing (14).
* Walking blamelessly and innocently in the world so that you can shine (15).
* Holding fast to Jesus and the Bible (16).
* Loving God and loving people for the glory of God (17).

PHILIPPIANS 3
PRESS ON!

I have mentioned already that one of the psychological tests the Army would do in the US Army Ranger School would be to give us false finish lines and then push us past them. This was done in various ways, whether it involved pushing us through very long nights and days of movements with heavy equipment loads on our backs, or on routine runs that did not end when expected, or hours on the rocks training our bodies. All of this physical work was really mental work, training us to persevere and be resilient.

The book of Philippians was my favorite book in the Bible when I was going through Ranger School. My experience in a military school and the reality of our circumstances amid the COVID-19 pandemic both point me toward this word from Paul. Paul clearly expressed a focused tenacity to accomplish his life ambition in Philippians 3:10-14:

> That I may know Him and the power of His resurrection and the fellowship of His sufferings, being conformed to His death; in order that I may attain to the resurrection from the dead. Not that I have already obtained it or have already become perfect, but I press on so that I may lay hold of that for which also I was laid hold of by Christ Jesus. Brethren, I do not regard myself as having laid hold of it yet; but one thing I do: forgetting what lies behind and reaching forward to what lies ahead, I press on toward the goal for the prize of the upward call of God in Christ Jesus.

Seize the moment and press on to the goal of becoming like Jesus! This moment is a great opportunity; don't waste it! Persevere!

PHILIPPIANS 4
SPIRITUAL NUTRITION!

Nutrition is important—not only in your physical diet, but also in your spiritual life.

Just like it matters what you put into your body through your mouth, it matters what you put into your mind, heart, and soul through your eyes and ears. It matters what you think about, what you say, and what you do.

Let's learn some spiritual nutrition guidelines for healthy living from the final chapter of Paul's letter to the Philippians:

1. **Serve everything up with joy!** Paul testifies in Philippians 4:4, "Rejoice in the Lord always; again I will say, rejoice."

2. **Salt everything with thankfulness!** Paul commands in verses 6-7, "Be anxious for nothing, but in everything by prayer and supplication with thanksgiving let your requests be made known to God. And the peace of God, which surpasses all comprehension, will guard your hearts and your minds in Christ Jesus."

3. **Think healthy thoughts!** Paul teaches in verse 8, "Finally, brethren, whatever is true, whatever is honorable, whatever is right, whatever is pure, whatever is lovely, whatever is of good repute, if there is any excellence and if anything worthy of praise, dwell on these things."

4. **Be satisfied with what you are served!** Paul witnesses in verses 12-13, "I know how to get along with humble means, and I also know how to live in prosperity; in any and every circumstance I have learned the secret of being filled and going hungry, both of having abundance and suffering need. I can do all things through Him who strengthens me."

5. **Trust God for your daily bread!** Paul concludes with verse 19, "And my God will supply all your needs according to His riches in glory in Christ Jesus."

Seize the moment and focus on your spiritual nutrition!

COLOSSIANS 1
PROMINENT VS. PREEMINENT!

I want to introduce you to a big word we rarely use—preeminent.

Listen to Paul use this word in Colossians 1:15-20 (ESV),

He is the image of the invisible God, the firstborn of all creation. For by him all things were created, in heaven and on earth, visible and invisible, whether thrones or dominions or rulers or authorities—all things were created through him and for him. And he is before all things, and in him all things hold together. And he is the head of the body, the church. He is the beginning, the firstborn from the dead, that in everything he might be preeminent. For in him all the fullness of God was pleased to dwell, and through him to reconcile to himself all things, whether on earth or in heaven, making peace by the blood of his cross.

In other translations, "preeminent" is replaced by, "first place in everything" (NAS95) and "supremacy" (NIV).

In other words, to be preeminent means that God wins in all things and His ways rule the world.

Is Jesus *prominent* in a few areas of your life, or *preeminent* over your entire life? Another way to ask that question is: Do you want to be a fan or a follower of Jesus?

There is a chasm between the two. One leads to rest and the other to frustration. One is under grace and the other is under the law.

Jesus always has been, and always will be, preeminent. The question is: to what extent do you acknowledge that truth and live according to what you say you believe?

Seize the moment and fully surrender to Jesus' preeminence.

COLOSSIANS 2
INVITATION TO RELATIONSHIP!

It is my greatest desire that you will be a follower of Jesus!

Paul explains in Colossians 2:20-23,

If you have died with Christ to the elementary principles of the world, why, as if you were living in the world, do you submit yourself to decrees, such as, "Do not handle, do not taste, do not touch!" (which all refer to things destined to perish with use)—in accordance with the commandments and teachings of men? These are matters which have, to be sure, the appearance of wisdom in self-made religion and self-abasement and severe treatment of the body, but are of no value against fleshly indulgence.

Paul states the uselessness of "self-made religion." To be completely transparent, I'm not interested in leading us in, or passing on to others, that which does not work, simply for the sake of tradition. Only Jesus saves!

So, as Paul did for the followers of Jesus in Colossae, I pray Paul's prayer from Colossians 2:6-10 for you today:

Therefore as you have received Christ Jesus the Lord, so walk in Him, having been firmly rooted and now being built up in Him and established in your faith, just as you were instructed, and overflowing with gratitude. See to it that no one takes you captive through philosophy and empty deception, according to the tradition of men, according to the elementary principles of the world, rather than according to Christ. For in Him all the fullness of Deity dwells in bodily form, and in Him you have been made complete, and He is the head over all rule and authority.

May we each, through time spent with the Living God in prayer and study of His Word, know the difference between the trappings of man-made religion and the promises of God-given relationship.

Seize the moment and follow Jesus. Spend time with Him today.

COLOSSIANS 3
PUT OFF THE OLD TO PUT ON THE NEW!

Have you ever seen a house where the owners kept putting on layers of new shingles on the roof without taking off the old?

If you don't discard the old before you put on the new, you may still end up with a leaky roof! You have to get underneath the surface to deal with the issue.

Listen to Paul teach about putting off the old in Colossians 3:8-10:

But now you also, put them all aside: anger, wrath, malice, slander, and abusive speech from your mouth. Do not lie to one another, since you laid aside the old self with its evil practices, and have put on the new self who is being renewed to a true knowledge according to the image of the One who created him.

Just like with a new roof, the new life in Christ is a partnership with the Holy Spirit to take off the old, deal with what is underneath the surface, and put on the new!

Here are three daily steps to remember:

1. **Invite the Holy Spirit!** Recognize you can't do it on your own so invite the God to be your general contractor. Pray!

2. **Get Into God's Word!** It is through the Bible that the Holy Spirit will direct your steps, ensuring the old is taken off and the new is being put on according to God's plans.

3. **Make a Commitment!** Remain faithful day in and day out during this construction project. This is a long slow obedience in the same direction. Don't bail before the blessing!

Seize the moment and be transformed through God's grace! We can do nothing apart from Him (John 15:5).

COLOSSIANS 4
CLEAR COMMANDS FOR THE CHRISTIAN LIFE!

Here are Paul's final instructions to the followers of Jesus in Colossae, found in Colossians 4:2-6:

> Devote yourselves to prayer, keeping alert in it with an attitude of thanksgiving; praying at the same time for us as well, that God will open up to us a door for the word, so that we may speak forth the mystery of Christ, for which I have also been imprisoned; that I may make it clear in the way I ought to speak. Conduct yourselves with wisdom toward outsiders, making the most of the opportunity. Let your speech always be with grace, as though seasoned with salt, so that you will know how you should respond to each person.

Paul's desire in each of his letters to the local churches, and local church leaders, was to encourage their daily lives so that they walked in a manner worthy of the Gospel of Jesus Christ.

Allow me to summarize Paul's clear commands of how to walk faithfully in Christ:

1. Be devoted (steadfast) in your prayers.
2. Look for God in all of your circumstances and give thanks to Him for His presence.
3. Be ready, with eyes wide open, for opportunities to love people in word and deed in the name of Jesus Christ.
4. Make the most of every circumstance, remembering that every crisis is an opportunity.
5. Salt everything with God's grace and truth. Love others as God loves you—through grace and forgiveness; please be gentle with one another.

This seems to be a theme! Paul has given us very clear commands on how we are to live our faith as followers of Jesus—we are to rejoice always, pray without ceasing, and give thanks in all circumstances.

Seize the moment and walk in this way.

1 & 2
THESSALONIANS

1 THESSALONIANS 1
A GREAT RECIPE FOR CHRISTIAN LIVING!

Do you like to cook? Do you follow recipes, or create your own along the way?

Either way, you know that the finished product depends on getting all the ingredients just right. If you are missing something, the meal may be "good enough," but it won't be great!

Paul teaches in 1 Thessalonians 1:4-7,

Knowing, brethren beloved by God, His choice of you; for our gospel did not come to you in word only, but also in power and in the Holy Spirit and with full conviction; just as you know what kind of men we proved to be among you for your sake. You also became imitators of us and of the Lord, having received the word in much tribulation with the joy of the Holy Spirit, so that you became an example to all the believers in Macedonia and in Achaia.

Paul gives us God's recipe for all disciples to live in such a way that we line up with the gospel of Jesus Christ:

1. **Our lives align with the Word of God!** His Word is a lamp unto our feet and a light unto our path (Psalm 119:105).
2. **Our lives manifest the power of God!** We overcome by the blood of the Lamb and the word of our testimony (Revelation 12:11).
3. **Our lives are directed by the Holy Spirit!** The Holy Spirit is not only the sustainer of all Christian life, but He is also the teacher of God's Word, and the guide for using God's power (John 14:26).
4. **Our lives are anchored with a deep conviction!** Our only certainty for this life, and life eternal, is our faith and hope in Jesus Christ (Hebrews 11:1-6).

This is the perfect recipe for living the victorious Christian life. Are you missing any of the ingredients?

Seize the moment and follow the recipe for godly living! You don't have to settle for "good enough."

1 THESSALONIANS 2
INFLUENCE THE NEXT GENERATION!

Do you want to be a great parent? Did you know that one of the clearest New Testament teachings on parenting is found in 1 Thessalonians 2?

For moms, Paul says in verses 7-10,

> But we proved to be gentle among you, as a nursing mother tenderly cares for her own children. Having so fond an affection for you, we were well-pleased to impart to you not only the gospel of God but also our own lives, because you had become very dear to us. For you recall, brethren, our labor and hardship, how working night and day so as not to be a burden to any of you, we proclaimed to you the gospel of God. You are witnesses, and so is God, how devoutly and uprightly and blamelessly we behaved toward you believers.

Ladies, I encourage you to study this passage; get together and discuss it with one another.

For dads, Paul continues in verses 11-12, "Just as you know how we were exhorting and encouraging and imploring each one of you as a father would his own children, so that you would walk in a manner worthy of the God who calls you into His own kingdom and glory."

Gentlemen, I encourage you to study this passage; get together and discuss it with one another.

Let me emphasize verse 10, which applies to all of us: be models of devout, upright, and blameless conduct before all the children.

Did you know that a majority of the next generation's learning about how to do life, relationships, marriage, and parenting (all the big important stuff) doesn't happen at school, but comes from watching you?

So, does it matter, then, how we live at home and at church? Yes, because little eyes are watching, and little ears are listening.

Seize the moment and live a biblical lifestyle today.

1 THESSALONIANS 3
STRENGTH IN THE FIGHT!

Paul's third chapter to the Thessalonians talks about how Paul was concerned that the "tempter" had worked to make his efforts "in vain" in the lives of the congregation (1 Thessalonians 3:5). This remains a real concern for church leadership to this day.

The spiritual reality is that the church lives continuously with a clear and present danger. We can expect afflictions in this life, and the devil (the tempter) is always on the prowl looking for his next victim to devour (1 Peter 5:8). The key to withstanding this clear and present danger is having a real, personal relationship with God through Jesus Christ.

That is why each of us are invited into a daily time with God in His Word: studying it, memorizing it, praying it, and applying into our everyday lives.

These daily devotions are designed to encourage you, to help you keep your eyes on Jesus, and to spur you on to remain effective in your Christian life. I want to care for the spiritual well-being of God's people the best way I know how—following the teaching of the New Testament and as modeled by the apostles: "We will devote ourselves to prayer and to the ministry of the word" (Acts 6:4).

So, as Paul prayed for the believers in Thessalonica in 1 Thessalonians 3:11-13, receive this prayer in the Spirit for your life today:

Now may our God and Father Himself and Jesus our Lord direct our way to you; and may the Lord cause you to increase and abound in love for one another, and for all people, just as we also do for you; so that He may establish your hearts without blame in holiness before our God and Father at the coming of our Lord Jesus with all His saints.

Seize the moment and find strength for today by meeting with God—in His Word and in prayer with Him.

1 THESSALONIANS 4
PRACTICAL WISDOM FOR TODAY!

Does the Bible give practical wisdom for your everyday life?

Listen to Paul teach in 1 Thessalonians 4:9-12,

Now as to the love of the brethren, you have no need for anyone to write to you, for you yourselves are taught by God to love one another; for indeed you do practice it toward all the brethren who are in all Macedonia. But we urge you, brethren, to excel still more, and to make it your ambition to lead a quiet life and attend to your own business and work with your hands, just as we commanded you, so that you will behave properly toward outsiders and not be in any need.

Paul gives four practical points of advice for how we are to live the Christian life:

1. **Be healthy in your relationships!** The proof of our love for God is how we love one another. The purity of our "love of the brethren" (9) is the evidence of our sanctification (3).
2. **Focus your life's message!** When we "lead a quiet life" (11), we are not hiding our light under a bushel; rather, we are focusing our life on the gospel. We are turning down the ambient light of our lives, so that what people see and hear from us is the gospel!
3. **Be emotionally healthy!** God cares that we "attend to [our] own business" (11). Being a gossip, or needing to know information about other people's lives, distracts you and detracts from your ability to be in God's will in your own life.
4. **Work with a purpose!** The ability to "work with [our] hands" (11) is a gift from God and He cares that, whatever we do, we do our work with your whole heart to His glory.

We are to follow these four teachings "so that [we] will behave properly toward outsiders and not be in any need" (12). It's all for God's glory!

Seize the moment and shine His light by the way you live your everyday life.

1 THESSALONIANS 5
THE HOPE OF THE SECOND ADVENT!

The teachings of the Advent of Jesus' Second Coming were intended to focus believers and unify them with faith, hope, and love as they faced the trials and tribulations of the day.

Listen to Paul teach these truths in 1 Thessalonians 5:1-11:

Now as to the times and the epochs, brethren, you have no need of anything to be written to you. For you yourselves know full well that the day of the Lord will come just like a thief in the night. While they are saying, "Peace and safety!" then destruction will come upon them suddenly like labor pains upon a woman with child, and they will not escape. But you, brethren, are not in darkness, that the day would overtake you like a thief; for you are all sons of light and sons of day. ... But since we are of the day, let us be sober, having put on the breastplate of faith and love, and as a helmet, the hope of salvation. For God has not destined us for wrath, but for obtaining salvation through our Lord Jesus Christ, who died for us, so that whether we are awake or asleep, we will live together with Him. Therefore encourage one another and build up one another, just as you also are doing.

Here are two things to know about the Second Advent of Christ:

1. **The timing of Jesus' second coming is imminent!** It's a future hope that has great implications on our everyday faith! The Day of the Lord is to focus our hearts and minds on Jesus, keeping Him preeminent in our lives no matter what is happening today.

2. **The anticipation determines how we live today!** We are to let our lives visibly manifest the love of God. Jesus came to bring light into the world; until His return, we are His light-bearers to the world.

Seize the moment and shine brightly. Live a life of faith and love, rooted in your Advent hope.

2 THESSALONIANS 1
GIVE THANKS AND PRAY FOR ONE ANOTHER!

What does it feel like to have someone in your corner—someone who believes in you and is thankful for you; someone who prays for you?

I think this is one of the major needs that has been revealed through the reality of the COVID-19 pandemic. We are struggling in our well-being because many of us are cut off from normal social rhythms, like going to church. We are easy prey to the devil when we actively feed the feelings that we are alone, isolated, or unwanted.

There is a solution, friend!

Paul starts his second letter to the believers in Thessalonica with thanksgiving for them. Listen to 2 Thessalonians 1:3, "We ought always to give thanks to God for you, brethren, as is only fitting, because your faith is greatly enlarged, and the love of each one of you toward one another grows ever greater."

The solution is you being the Church—Paul knows we are better together, and it takes each of us growing in our faith for all of us to be healthy. When you pray and take the initiative to serve another, then you get blessed in return.

Are you feeling alone and unwanted? Rebuke those lies by calling someone and giving thanks for them today! Be a part of the solution by being a blessing today.

Receive this prayer for you from verses 11-12, "To this end also we pray for you always, that our God will count you worthy of your calling, and fulfill every desire for goodness and the work of faith with power, so that the name of our Lord Jesus will be glorified in you, and you in Him, according to the grace of our God and the Lord Jesus Christ."

Amen!

Seize the moment and be the Church you so desperately want your church to be.

2 THESSALONIANS 2
STAND FIRM IN DIFFICULT AND DARK DAYS!

Do you need help in standing firm in difficult and dark days? Are current events shaking your faith, or distracting you from the hope we have in God's promises?

Listen to Paul's encouraging words from 2 Thessalonians 2:13-15:

But we should always give thanks to God for you, brethren beloved by the Lord, because God has chosen you from the beginning for salvation through sanctification by the Spirit and faith in the truth. It was for this He called you through our gospel, that you may gain the glory of our Lord Jesus Christ. So then, brethren, stand firm and hold to the traditions which you were taught, whether by word of mouth or by letter from us.

It is important to note that Paul gave these encouraging words after a very hard teaching on the end times in verses 1-12. Those twelve verses are sobering to all; for many, they are confusing.

Notice that the first word of verse 13, after such a difficult teaching, is "But."

Paul transitions to encourage the believers: no matter what may be happening, or will be happening, in this world, you, beloved of God, stand firm in what God has done, is doing, and will do. Trust God, you chosen of God, and stand firm in difficult and dark days!

Allow me to pray Paul's prayer over you, from verses 16-17, "Now may our Lord Jesus Christ Himself and God our Father, who has loved us and given us eternal comfort and good hope by grace, comfort and strengthen your hearts in every good work and word." Amen.

Seize the moment and stand firm no matter how dark or difficult the day.

2 THESSALONIANS 3
PERSEVERANCE!

Do you have perseverance?

Paul prayed this for the followers of Jesus in 2 Thessalonians 3:5, "May the Lord direct your hearts into the love of God and into the steadfastness of Christ." The NIV says it this way, "May the Lord direct your hearts into God's love and Christ's perseverance."

What is perseverance?

Biblically, perseverance is endurance in spite of opposition. It's the condition of, and the action of, steadfastness. That is why Paul not only prays for this condition to be in the saints of God, but also then commands them in verse 13, "brethren, do not grow weary of doing good."

Remember how Paul started the letter in 2 Thessalonians 1:3-4,

We ought always to give thanks to God for you, brethren, as is only fitting, because your faith is greatly enlarged, and the love of each one of you toward one another grows ever greater; therefore, we ourselves speak proudly of you among the churches of God for your perseverance and faith in the midst of all your persecutions and afflictions which you endure.

So, here is the key: perseverance is both a *condition* given to you by the faithfulness of God and an *action* empowered unto you by the faithfulness of God.

Paul reinforces the need for perseverance in his benediction in 2 Thessalonians 3:16, "Now may the Lord of peace Himself continually grant you peace in every circumstance. The Lord be with you all!"

Seize the moment and be at peace: The Lord will persevere in and through you. Rest in His easy yoke.

1 & 2
TIMOTHY,
TITUS, AND
PHILEMON

1 TIMOTHY 1
THE POWER OF TESTIMONY!

This morning, I had the privilege of reviewing a five-minute video testimony that one of our church members made for this coming Sunday's service. She made this video to share God's hope with all of us—to remind us that, even when life and circumstances are hard, God is faithful and loving. I love it when people share their testimonies. It fills me with faith, hope, and love.

Listen to the Apostle Paul share his testimony in 1 Timothy 1:12-17:

I thank Christ Jesus our Lord, who has strengthened me, because He considered me faithful, putting me into service, even though I was formerly a blasphemer and a persecutor and a violent aggressor. Yet I was shown mercy because I acted ignorantly in unbelief; and the grace of our Lord was more than abundant, with the faith and love which are found in Christ Jesus. It is a trustworthy statement, deserving full acceptance, that Christ Jesus came into the world to save sinners, among whom I am foremost of all. Yet for this reason I found mercy, so that in me as the foremost, Jesus Christ might demonstrate His perfect patience as an example for those who would believe in Him for eternal life. Now to the King eternal, immortal, invisible, the only God, be honor and glory forever and ever. Amen.

Did you see how Paul, in finishing his testimony, praised God?

Remembering what God had done for him in the past, Paul was moved to thank God in the present. Paul's testimony has given so many people hope; if God can love and forgive Paul, then, yes, God can love and forgive me too.

That is the power of testimony!

Seize the moment and share your testimony—give the gift of faith, hope, and love to another person.

1 TIMOTHY 2
YOUR TOP CIVIC RESPONSIBILITY!

What is your top civic responsibility as a Christian?

Paul wrote this passage at a time when the Roman government was far from favorable to him or to the cause of the Christian church. In fact, the authorities he is talking about in this passage have imprisoned him and would soon kill him for his faith. Understanding this should change the way we read this passage; we are called to sacrificial love as citizens of any nation.

Paul commands all of us in 1 Timothy 2:1-6,

First of all, then, I urge that entreaties and prayers, petitions and thanksgivings, be made on behalf of all men, for kings and all who are in authority, so that we may lead a tranquil and quiet life in all godliness and dignity. This is good and acceptable in the sight of God our Savior, who desires all men to be saved and to come to the knowledge of the truth. For there is one God, and one mediator also between God and men, the man Christ Jesus, who gave Himself as a ransom for all, the testimony given at the proper time.

Your top civic responsibility is to pray! These prayers are not just for the highest officials in the government, but also for those you are called to be civil with, like your neighbor, or your coworker, or the person sitting across the pew from you.

This civic responsibility is a commanded way of life in the Bible; it is the way for having right relationships with other people, the truth for right interpretations of your circumstances, and the life for effectively expressing your faith in Jesus to the world.

Seize the moment and pray! God has strategically placed you in your community to pray and live a life of sacrificial love.

1 TIMOTHY 3
THE MYSTERY OF GODLINESS!

Have you ever noticed Paul's beautiful doxology, or song of praise, at the end of 1 Timothy 3?

Listen to it in verse 16, "By common confession, great is the mystery of godliness: He who was revealed in the flesh, was vindicated in the Spirit, seen by angels, proclaimed among the nations, believed on in the world, taken up in glory."

This was an early creed of the New Testament Church, used to teach their faith and shape their communities.

The mystery of godliness encompasses Jesus' miraculous birth, His perfect life, His sacrificial death, His victorious resurrection, His triumphant ascension, and His imminent second coming. We are to proclaim this!

The mystery of godliness was made visible to us in the miracle of Christmas. It is revealed in the incarnation—that the God who is Spirit would dwell fully in human flesh as a baby.

God chose to reveal His majesty to us by becoming one of us, in a particular form, in a specific time and space. God became one of us, as a human baby, and became completely dependent on His creatures for His care and well-being—for His survival.

God continues to trust us to fulfill His mission to preach the good news of His coming to the world so that all the nations can know what is the mystery of godliness.

Seize the moment and proclaim the mystery of godliness through a song of praise!

1 TIMOTHY 4
TRAIN YOURSELF FOR GODLINESS!

Have you ever met someone who lives in the past—a person who feels that the best is behind them and doesn't have hope for the future?

Paul teaches us in 1 Timothy 4:7b-10,

On the other hand, discipline yourself for the purpose of godliness; for bodily discipline is only of little profit, but godliness is profitable for all things, since it holds promise for the present life and also for the life to come. It is a trustworthy statement deserving full acceptance. For it is for this we labor and strive, because we have fixed our hope on the living God, who is the Savior of all men, especially of believers.

I can testify to you that physical training does have a season of glory, whether that season ends in high school, college, the Olympics, or professional sports, but there is a day where even the most celebrated athlete's career must come to an end. As the sun sets on any athletic season, what do those athletes have left? Who are they, apart from their accomplishments and accolades?

Here is the good news: **When we train ourselves in godliness, the best is always yet to come!** The glory days are never behind us, but always before us! When you train yourself according to the Word of God, the living God sets before you a future that has the truest and highest honor of being welcomed into the victor's circle of Heaven (1 Corinthians 9:25).

Seize the moment and train yourself in godliness. This way, you'll always have your best days ahead of you.

1 TIMOTHY 5
THE BASICS OF THE CHRISTIAN LIFE!

When I was in the Army, we would conduct basic infantry "battle drills" all the time. The battle drills are the building blocks of individual skills and responsibilities on the battlefield—how to shoot, move, and communicate. Battle drills were drilled into us because people tend to forget how to do the basics well when under stress.

As a pastor, part of my responsibility is to lead people through battle drills of the Christian life, so that we do the basics well, even when we are under stress.

As I read my Bible this morning, I am reminded of the simple wisdom of getting back to the basics. Paul said to Timothy in 1 Timothy 5:1-2, "Do not sharply rebuke an older man, but rather appeal to him as a father, to the younger men as brothers, the older women as mothers, and the younger women as sisters, in all purity."

Here are a few basics for us:

1. Do not "sharply rebuke" (be harsh with) the elderly, but rather encourage them. Treat older men as you would your father, and older women as your mother. In other words, honor the elderly in our midst for their wisdom and life experiences.

2. Treat people your own age and younger as your brothers and sisters "in all purity." In other words, do not objectify and use one another, but recognize the value and worth in one another as human beings and treat each other accordingly.

3. These basic practices extend beyond the church; we are to extend these graces to others. What a great witness that would be to our world today!

Seize the moment and get back to the basics. Practice them in every part of your life, so that when stress comes, only love and the fruit of the Spirit come out of you in word and deed.

1 TIMOTHY 6
GODLINESS WITH CONTENTMENT!

Are you content?

Paul states in 1 Timothy 6:6, "But godliness with contentment is great gain" (ESV).

When you look at the context of this verse, we learn that we are to pursue "godliness," which is the work of the Holy Spirit in us to conform us into the image of Christ. Christlikeness restores us as the Image Bearers of God to the world. Part of this pursuit is remaining content in the midst of both religious (3-5) and worldly power plays (7-10), both of which lead to discontentment.

Then, Paul writes in verses 11-16,

> But flee from these things, you man of God, and pursue righteousness, godliness, faith, love, perseverance and gentleness. Fight the good fight of faith; take hold of the eternal life to which you were called, and you made the good confession in the presence of many witnesses. I charge you in the presence of God, who gives life to all things, and of Christ Jesus, who testified the good confession before Pontius Pilate, that you keep the commandment without stain or reproach until the appearing of our Lord Jesus Christ, which He will bring about at the proper time— He who is the blessed and only Sovereign, the King of kings and Lord of lords, who alone possesses immortality and dwells in unapproachable light, whom no man has seen or can see. To Him be honor and eternal dominion! Amen.

Seize the moment and pursue a growing relationship with Jesus with all of your heart, soul, mind, and strength. We have much to gain in godliness through contentment in all things. When we seek first the Kingdom of God, and His righteousness, Jesus promises to lead us into His abundant life.

2 TIMOTHY 1
THE PRIORITY AT HOME!

What are the priorities of your home life?

Listen to 2 Timothy 1:5-7,

For I am mindful of the sincere faith within you, which first dwelt in your grandmother Lois and your mother Eunice, and I am sure that it is in you as well. For this reason I remind you to kindle afresh the gift of God which is in you through the laying on of my hands. For God has not given us a spirit of timidity, but of power and love and discipline.

Paul is reminded of Timothy's sincere faith, a faith that now dwells in him, but started in his childhood home. Even though Paul and Timothy grew up in very different circumstances and cultures, Paul praised Timothy's upbringing because it was one of faith.

So often in American culture, we are expected to fill kids' time with new experiences and activities, ensuring they have every opportunity, in hopes they will be successful in the future.

However, do we neglect the simple things that our children really need? A home that is a sanctuary of faith, hope, and love. A home that is a safe place where they feel secure, where their souls can find rest, where their minds and hearts are guarded by the peace of God. A home that is filled with the care and concern that comes from God through our healthy relationships.

If you desire to give your kids the very best, then make your home a safe place of refuge and protection. This is not to hide them from the world, but rather to create a place of intentional preparation for what is to come: a life of service to Jesus Christ.

Seize the moment and prioritize Jesus in your life and home today. Children learn by watching the adults in their lives!

2 TIMOTHY 2
PURSUE THE DEEPER LIFE WITH JESUS!

You have heard of "stop, drop, and roll!" when you are on fire. Well, I say to you: "stop, turn (away), and run (into the arms of Jesus)!" when you are finding yourself struggling in life.

Paul teaches us in 2 Timothy 2:22-26,

Now flee from youthful lusts and pursue righteousness, faith, love and peace, with those who call on the Lord from a pure heart. But refuse foolish and ignorant speculations, knowing that they produce quarrels. The Lord's bond-servant must not be quarrelsome, but be kind to all, able to teach, patient when wronged, with gentleness correcting those who are in opposition, if perhaps God may grant them repentance leading to the knowledge of the truth, and they may come to their senses and escape from the snare of the devil, having been held captive by him to do his will.

The Bible diagnoses us as having been given over to our passions and desires, and that breeds quarrels within us! When your desire for anything outweighs your desire for God, there is war! When you desire to break your promises with others in hopes of finding personal fulfillment, there is war! When you struggle to love and trust, there is war!

There is only one hope for victory; He is the living hope—our hope is found in a personal relationship with Jesus Christ!

Decide today to move away from what "produce quarrels" (**Stop!**), flee from all immorality (**Turn Away!**), and pursue Jesus Christ in righteousness, faith, love, and peace (**Run into the Arms of Jesus!**).

Seize the moment and make it your all-consuming ambition to live a victorious life for God by pursuing the deeper life with Jesus Christ.

2 TIMOTHY 3
THE WORD OF GOD!

Paul exhorts his disciple Timothy in 2 Timothy 3:16-17, "All Scripture is inspired by God and profitable for teaching, for reproof, for correction, for training in righteousness; so that the man [and woman] of God may be adequate, equipped for every good work."

Over the years of the hard and messy hands-on work of helping people in their very real situations in a very broken world, I have been deeply converted to the power of God's Word, not as a propositional truth, but as a living truth. When my words go dry, there is a deep well of wisdom in the Bible. When a situation presents itself with no hope, there is still reason to hope in Jesus.

The Bible accurately diagnoses and effectively treats us. We each need the right kind of help and we each can get world-class care from the Wonderful Counselor and Mighty Physician. Turn to Jesus today, open His love letter to you (the Bible), and find rest for your souls. As He quiets the storm inside of you, you will see a new way through your circumstances. The Word of God does not return void—it illuminates the way to peace and wholeness!

I encourage you to pray this prayer today: Lord, You teach us that Your Word will never return void, so I pray that You will plant the good seeds of Your Word deep into my heart and mind that it would bear good fruit in me, deliver and rescue me, heal and transform my life. In Jesus' name. Amen.

Seize the moment and re-commit yourself, and your family, to daily time with Jesus by opening your Bible to read and pray God's Word.

2 TIMOTHY 4
BUT YOU!

Whenever we examine our surrounding circumstances, it is easy to become discouraged by things out of your control or get distracted by all the voices and actions of people around you.

In 2 Timothy 4:1-4 (ESV), we read Paul's exhortation to Timothy,

I give you this charge: Preach the Word; be prepared in season and out of season; correct, rebuke and encourage—with great patience and careful instruction. For the time will come when men will not put up with sound doctrine. Instead, to suit their own desires, they will gather around them a great number of teachers to say what their itching ears want to hear. They will turn their ears away from the truth and turn aside to myths. But you, keep your head in all situations, endure hardship, do the work of an evangelist, discharge all the duties of your ministry.

After very clearly charging and warning Timothy, Paul says to him, "But you …"

You have heard me say that the two most powerful words in the Bible are, "But God …" No matter our situations, we can trust God. As those words, "But God …" become the bedrock of our lives, we can then live out Paul's "But you …" in his final words to Timothy.

Other people are saying or doing things the world's way, "But you …"

Current events and lack of control foster anxiety, "But you …"

You, stay focused on what God has given you to do. Jesus once said this very same thing to a very distracted Peter, "… what is that to you? You follow Me!" (John 21:22).

Seize the moment and remain faithful to God's call on your life amid all the distractions.

TITUS 1
PASS THE BATON!

Moses did it! Elijah did it! Jesus did it! Paul did it!

Are you doing it?

Right about now you are thinking, what do these four famous people from Bible history have in common? What did they each do?

Moses equipped and empowered Joshua! Elijah equipped and empowered Elisha! Jesus equipped and empowered the Apostles! Paul equipped and empowered Timothy and Titus!

They all trained up and passed on authority to younger leaders; they passed the baton!

One of my favorite leadership verses in the Bible is 2 Timothy 2:2, "The things which you have heard from me in the presence of many witnesses, entrust to faithful men [and women] who will be able to teach others also."

Paul gave Titus a very similar command in Titus 1:5, "For this reason I left you in Crete, that you would set in order what remains and appoint elders in every city as I directed you." Paul has passed the baton to Titus, so that Titus will pass the baton to others who are qualified to lead (Titus 1:6-9).

If you say that you are not being fed, it is because you have not grown up yet! You may have gained a base of knowledge that has given you an insatiable appetite for knowledge, but the reason you are not being fed is because you are not designed to eat and eat and eat; that will only make you sick (the Bible calls it the sickness of being "puffed up" … prideful)! You are designed to pass the baton to others. If you want to grow up, you must do what Moses, Elijah, Jesus, and Paul did! You must pass it on by training up and teaching others what you have been taught.

Seize the moment and pass on your faith to another. Mentor someone in the faith this year. Pass the baton!

TITUS 2
A GOSPEL MOVEMENT!

God does not call us to build a monument to Jesus, but, rather, a movement of people who proclaim the gospel of Jesus. How are we invited, by God's Word, to invest in people?

Men and women alike, younger and older, we are all invited to hear the invitation.

Listen to Titus 2:3-8,

Older women likewise are to be reverent in their behavior, not malicious gossips nor enslaved to much wine, teaching what is good, so that they may encourage the young women to love their husbands, to love their children, to be sensible, pure, workers at home, kind, being subject to their own husbands, so that the word of God will not be dishonored. Likewise urge the young men to be sensible; in all things show yourself to be an example of good deeds, with purity in doctrine, dignified, sound in speech which is beyond reproach, so that the opponent will be put to shame, having nothing bad to say about us.

What do we have that we can invest in other people?

Here are a few ideas to help you to start to think about how God is inviting you to be part of this movement:

1. **Your time!** This is the most limited, and, therefore, the most precious of our resources.

2. **Your money!** Your heart follows your money. Be careful of where you lead your heart with how you invest your money!

3. **Your heart!** Talk about a precious and very limited resource. Love is your greatest enterprise, and your greatest risk.

4. **Your mind!** Start training your mind with God's Word so that you can invest your mental energy on what matters most in life.

Seize the moment and invest in the movement of the gospel of Jesus today. Pour all that you have into the eternal work of people.

TITUS 3
A GOSPEL REMINDER IN DARK DAYS!

It is my privilege and joy to remind you of the gospel of Jesus Christ, which is the good news of great joy to all people, in the midst of a constant stream of bad news.

Paul reminds Titus of the grace of God in Titus 3:3-7:

For we also once were foolish ourselves, disobedient, deceived, enslaved to various lusts and pleasures, spending our life in malice and envy, hateful, hating one another. But when the kindness of God our Savior and His love for mankind appeared, He saved us, not on the basis of deeds which we have done in righteousness, but according to His mercy, by the washing of regeneration and renewing by the Holy Spirit, whom He poured out upon us richly through Jesus Christ our Savior, so that being justified by His grace we would be made heirs according to the hope of eternal life.

The gospel of Jesus Christ is good news; it is God's saving grace, God's richness of mercy, and God's goodness and loving-kindness toward people.

As we learn from Titus 3, the gospel is light in darkness; it is the "But God …" in any and every situation of our lives (cf. Ephesians 2:4-5; Romans 6:23).

As I wrote this, there were many reminders of the dark days we are in that we could have dwelt on: the political situation of our country, dangerous civil unrest, and the uncertainty of the COVID-19 pandemic, to name a few. But we have enough people talking about the problems.

I am called by God to unapologetically proclaim the solution of God and remind you of the unwavering hope of the gospel of Jesus Christ!

Seize the moment today, and every time you hear or read an unsettling news story. Declare to it: "But God!" My God is bigger!

PHILEMON
A TRANSFORMED STORY!

Change is hard, but the whole Christian life is about change—we are to be transformed through the renewal of our minds. This is demonstrated radically in the one-chapter book, Philemon. The purpose of Philemon is the redemption of a person's life, the transformation of a story.

When we are saved, how we view the world, and relate to ourselves and other people, begins to change. In this letter, Paul had to use his friendship and apostolic authority to get Philemon to stop thinking and behaving according to the political and economic patterns of this world and be transformed by the renewal of his mind (Romans 12:1-2).

Paul writes to Philemon about Onesimus in verses 10-16,

I appeal to you for my child Onesimus, whom I have begotten in my imprisonment, who formerly was useless to you, but now is useful both to you and to me. I have sent him back to you in person, that is, sending my very heart, whom I wished to keep with me, so that on your behalf he might minister to me in my imprisonment for the gospel; but without your consent I did not want to do anything, so that your goodness would not be, in effect, by compulsion but of your own free will. For perhaps he was for this reason separated from you for a while, that you would have him back forever, no longer as a slave, but more than a slave, a beloved brother, especially to me, but how much more to you, both in the flesh and in the Lord.

For you to truly live up to the radical call of Paul's letter to Philemon, regardless of whether you are young or old in the faith, you must invite the Holy Spirit to challenge you regarding what areas of modern life and thinking need to be transformed in you through the renewing of the mind, so that you start relating to people, and the world around you, like a child of God.

Seize the moment and remember who you are in Jesus: You are no longer a slave to fear, you are a child of God.

HEBREWS

HEBREWS 1
WORSHIP JESUS ABOVE ALL ELSE!

As I read Hebrews 1, there is one message that is clear: Jesus Christ is to be worshipped above all things in all of creation.

We see this in Hebrews 1:1-4:

God, after He spoke long ago to the fathers in the prophets in many portions and in many ways, in these last days has spoken to us in His Son, whom He appointed heir of all things, through whom also He made the world. And He is the radiance of His glory and the exact representation of His nature, and upholds all things by the word of His power. When He had made purification of sins, He sat down at the right hand of the Majesty on high, having become as much better than the angels, as He has inherited a more excellent name than they.

In this first chapter of Hebrews, the author quotes multiple Old Testament passages, including Psalm 104, to proclaim the awesomeness of God's splendor and majesty that has been made known and visible to us through Jesus Christ.

The point is that Jesus is greater than all of creation, including the angels, who people have wanted to worship throughout history, and even still today. Verse 14 teaches us that angels exist "to render service for the sake of those who will inherit salvation." The true purpose for all of creation, seen and unseen, is to bring glory to God so that we may know Him and enjoy Him forever.

Seize the moment and worship Jesus above all else; only He is worthy of your worship!

HEBREWS 2
MEDIC!

You have seen in the movies that when a soldier is wounded in battle, one of his buddies cries out, "medic!" What does the medic do? Often putting himself in great danger—he goes to the man down to give him aid.

Like a medic on the battlefield, Jesus left His place of safety to enter the battlefield of human life; He came from heaven to earth in order to provide aid to anyone who would call upon His name.

Hebrews 2:17-18 is a triumphant declaration of why Jesus Christ came into the world:

> Therefore, He had to be made like His brethren in all things, so that He might become a merciful and faithful high priest in things pertaining to God, to make propitiation for the sins of the people. For since He Himself was tempted in that which He has suffered, He is able to come to the aid of those who are tempted.

Do you need help with the temptations you are facing in your life? Are you struggling with issues of forgiveness in your relationships? Are you facing a health crisis, or financial difficulty?

Cry out to Jesus today and He will come to your aid!

The gospel is the story of the greatest rescue effort ever made in the history of humanity. Jesus came on a mission—to seek and to save that which was lost (Luke 19:10)!

Do you see someone else on the battlefield who is in need of Jesus' help and rescue?

You have been saved to be a part of the great rescue work of Jesus! You have been blessed to be a blessing! You have been empowered and equipped with the presence of God's Spirit in you!

Seize the moment and be the hands and feet of Jesus today. Pray for someone! Offer someone practical help today!

HEBREWS 3
HOLD FAST TO THE PROMISES OF GOD!

Today's reading in Hebrews 3 is a great reminder that God has given us the privilege of partaking in His nature according to the precious and magnificent promises of God.

Look at Hebrews 3:12-14:

Take care, brethren, that there not be in any one of you an evil, unbelieving heart that falls away from the living God. But encourage one another day after day, as long as it is still called "Today," so that none of you will be hardened by the deceitfulness of sin. For we have become partakers of Christ, if we hold fast the beginning of our assurance firm until the end.

The Bible commands us to live "today" with a present tense, active faith. We are called to watch our hearts and maintain our walks of faith—to hold fast! So, please, do not lose heart. Jesus will accomplish that which He promised; your deliverance is guaranteed, and your salvation is secured. God is faithful to keep all of His promises, and the grace of Jesus Christ is sufficient for you today!

Today is the day the Lord has made so let us rejoice and be glad in it! Remind yourself of this every morning, and it will change your outlook on your day more and more as you make it a habit of your life.

May the Holy Spirit remind you today of God's promise from Hebrews 3:6: "But Christ was faithful as a Son over His house—whose house we are, if we hold fast our confidence and the boast of our hope firm until the end." This is a promise with a practice—HOLD FAST!

Seize the moment—today is a great day to walk with Jesus! This is a key to victorious living—hold fast to the promises of God!

HEBREWS 4
DRAW NEAR!

How are you practically experiencing the promises of God in your daily life?

For example, in Matthew 11:28-30, Jesus promised that in His easy yoke all who are weary and heavy burdened will find rest.

God's word teaches us how this happens in Hebrews 4:11-13:

Therefore let us be diligent to enter that rest ... For the word of God is living and active and sharper than any two-edged sword, and piercing as far as the division of soul and spirit, of both joints and marrow, and able to judge the thoughts and intentions of the heart. And there is no creature hidden from His sight, but all things are open and laid bare to the eyes of Him with whom we have to do.

Here are three ways reading your Bible daily helps you enter into His rest:

1. There is great rest to be found in a personal relationship with God through Jesus Christ when we daily enter the rhythm of being still and knowing that He is God. It is wearisome trying to be God! He is God; we are not!

2. There is clarifying conviction that comes from reading His Word, because God knows us and our needs and sets us free from our burdens.

3. There is the Counselor's comfort when we invite the Holy Spirit to know our thoughts and hearts and speak truth to us.

Every day as you read and pray the Word of God, draw near to God; He promises to draw near to you (James 4:8).

Seize the moment and draw near today! Allow His Spirit to make you lie down in green pastures and lead you beside still waters (Psalm 23:2)—be diligent to enter His rest today.

HEBREWS 5
DISCERNMENT FOR TODAY!

There is more news and information available to people in today's world than ever before. This requires us to learn how to be discerning of what is good and what is evil.

Hebrews 5:12-14 teaches us about this:

For though by this time you ought to be teachers, you have need again for someone to teach you the elementary principles of the oracles of God, and you have come to need milk and not solid food. For everyone who partakes only of milk is not accustomed to the word of righteousness, for he is an infant. But solid food is for the mature, who because of practice have their senses trained to discern good and evil.

How do we grow in our ability to discern good and evil?

Developing and practicing discernment is a spiritual process led by the Holy Spirit, who uses the Word of God to cause you to become a person who knows the truth and knows what is good.

This comes from an intentional process of study and application; it is the integration of our minds and hearts, doctrines and practices, private life and public life. Discernment is trained through constant practice.

Churches in the midst of this information age will not mature in faithfulness and grow in fruitfulness without each of us becoming discerning members of His body. We all are overwhelmed with dissident information and competing ideas, and only those of us who choose obedience to Jesus Christ will ever become discerning of the things of God.

This is how we become wise! As Jesus taught us in Matthew 7:24, "Therefore everyone who hears these words of Mine and acts on them, may be compared to a wise man who built his house on the rock."

Seize the moment and build your house on the rock through daily study and application of God's Word.

HEBREWS 6
HOPE FOR THE FUTURE!

The Reverend Dr. Martin Luther King, Jr., a Baptist minister and recipient of the Nobel Peace Prize, is famously known for his 1963 "I Have a Dream" speech, when he said,

> Even though we face the difficulties of today and tomorrow, I still have a dream. It is a dream deeply rooted in the American dream. I have a dream that one day this nation will rise up and live out the true meaning of its creed: We hold these truths to be self-evident, that all men are created equal.[1]

Great leaders provide people with hope for a better future, especially in the midst of difficulties. Great leaders invite people to apply all diligence to bring about that future.

Hebrews 6:9-12, 19a teaches us to be diligent in the hope we have in Jesus Christ:

> But, beloved, we are convinced of better things concerning you, and things that accompany salvation, though we are speaking in this way. For God is not unjust so as to forget your work and the love which you have shown toward His name, in having ministered and in still ministering to the saints. And we desire that each one of you show the same diligence so as to realize the full assurance of hope until the end, so that you will not be sluggish, but imitators of those who through faith and patience inherit the promises. ... This hope we have as an anchor of the soul...

Anchor your life in the hope that only comes from Jesus Christ; He is your victory! Only through Him will you find peace of mind and heart, and rest for your soul. He's with you right now waiting for you to recognize His presence and call upon His name.

Seize the moment and be diligent to put all of your faith and hope in Jesus alone.

---

[1] King, Martin L. "I Have a Dream." Speech presented at the March on Washington for Jobs and Freedom, Washington, D.C., August 1963. https://avalon.law.yale.edu/20th_century/mlk01.asp.

HEBREWS 7
JESUS IS PRAYING FOR YOU!

Did you know that the most powerful intercessor in the world is praying perfectly for you, right now?

This is true for every believer in Christ Jesus. Listen to Hebrews 7:25-27:

Therefore He is able also to save forever those who draw near to God through Him, since He always lives to make intercession for them. For it was fitting for us to have such a high priest, holy, innocent, undefiled, separated from sinners and exalted above the heavens; who does not need daily, like those high priests, to offer up sacrifices, first for His own sins and then for the sins of the people, because this He did once for all when He offered up Himself.

Jesus is holy, innocent, without sin, separated from sinners, and exalted above the heavens.

Jesus is the High Priest, above all other priests, and His priesthood will never come to an end.

Jesus is the mediator and guarantor of the covenant of grace—and He is praying for you right now.

Paul explains this powerful prayer ministry of Jesus in Romans 8:33-35a, "Who will bring a charge against God's elect? God is the one who justifies; who is the one who condemns? Christ Jesus is He who died, yes, rather who was raised, who is at the right hand of God, who also intercedes for us. Who will separate us from the love of Christ?"

Just as the truth of God's forgiveness through the finished work of Jesus on the Cross of Calvary secures your eternal life, Jesus' promise for ongoing intercession at the throne of God's grace for secures your day-to-day life.

Seize the moment and join Jesus in His prayer life—partner in the life of Jesus by praying with Him! Never forget that Jesus is already praying for you!

HEBREWS 8
JESUS IS FAITHFUL TO HIS PROMISES!

Are you concerned that people will not keep their promises? This is a big concern in our culture today for many people.

Hebrews 8:6 teaches us about Jesus' covenant faithfulness: "But now He has obtained a more excellent ministry, by as much as He is also the mediator of a better covenant, which has been enacted on better promises."

God is faithful to His covenant—to His name! That is why He is faithful to you, not because you deserve it, but because of His name, His glory, His reputation!

Never forget that the promises of God are not dependent on your faithfulness, but on Jesus' faithfulness alone. In Christ alone, by faith, so that no man should boast.

When I think back to all of God's covenants, I come across this one truth: not a single one of those people was perfect, but God is!

Adam and Eve were not perfect. Neither were Noah, Abraham and Sarah, Israel and his twelve sons, King David … and the list goes on! Not a single perfect person in that group of people, only a perfect God!

Only Jesus Christ is perfect, and only Jesus mediates all of God's promises for imperfect people, like you and me! In God we trust! As a people, let's be honest about that and stop putting all of our hopes or fears in imperfect people!

Seize the moment and thank God for His grace available to imperfect people through faith in Jesus Christ! No human being alive can fully keep his or her promises, but God can!

HEBREWS 9
ONCE FOR ALL!

Why is Jesus so important two thousand years after He died?

According to Hebrews 9:11-12, it is *why* He died that makes Him relevant today:

> But when Christ appeared as a high priest of the good things to come, He entered through the greater and more perfect tabernacle, not made with hands, that is to say, not of this creation; and not through the blood of goats and calves, but through His own blood, He entered the holy place once for all, having obtained eternal redemption.

"Once" means that the atoning sacrifice for sin is done; the repetition of animal sacrifices demanded by the Old Covenant has been fulfilled through the one sacrifice of the Lamb of God, Jesus Christ. The New Covenant has been eternally sealed with His shed blood on the Cross.

"For all" means that Jesus has done this for all who shall be saved. This is the good news of great joy to all the world (Luke 2:10): God's promises are fulfilled in Jesus Christ and there is no end to His government (Isaiah 9:6-7)!

To drive home this point, look at Hebrews 9:27, "And inasmuch as it is appointed for men to die once and after this comes judgment."

It is an indisputable fact that every single one of us will die. The Bible further illuminates for our eternal good that each of us will face judgment after death. Your eternity—Heaven or Hell—is dependent on whether or not you call upon the name of the Lord to be saved (Romans 10:13).

Emphasizing the narrow path to Heaven is definitely out of fashion today, but that doesn't mean it's not relevant today!

Seize the moment and call upon the name of Jesus who died "once for all" so that you may be saved!

HEBREWS 10
LIVE BY FAITH!

God gives us two promises side by side in Hebrews 10; each of us has a choice to make. The first is for a wise person who builds life on the rock. Hebrews 10:19-25 teaches,

> Therefore, brethren, since we have confidence to enter the holy place by the blood of Jesus, by a new and living way which He inaugurated for us through the veil, that is, His flesh, and since we have a great priest over the house of God, let us draw near with a sincere heart in full assurance of faith, having our hearts sprinkled clean from an evil conscience and our bodies washed with pure water. Let us hold fast the confession of our hope without wavering, for He who promised is faithful; and let us consider how to stimulate one another to love and good deeds, not forsaking our own assembling together, as is the habit of some, but encouraging one another; and all the more as you see the day drawing near.

Contrast that with the person who builds life on the sand. Hebrews 10:26-31 continues,

> For if we go on sinning willfully after receiving the knowledge of the truth, there no longer remains a sacrifice for sins, but a terrifying expectation of judgment and the fury of a fire which will consume the adversaries. Anyone who has set aside the Law of Moses dies without mercy on the testimony of two or three witnesses. How much severer punishment do you think he will deserve who has trampled under foot the Son of God, and has regarded as unclean the blood of the covenant by which he was sanctified, and has insulted the Spirit of grace? For we know Him who said, "Vengeance is mine, I will repay." And again, "The LORD will judge His people." It is a terrifying thing to fall into the hands of the living God.

As a product of our free will, we choose to either live by faith or in fear.

Seize the moment and choose your response to the promises of God today.

HEBREWS 11
REAL LIFE STORIES OF FAITH!

According to Hebrews 11:1, faith is "the assurance of things hoped for, the conviction of things not seen." Verse 6 further explains that "without faith it is impossible to please Him, for he who comes to God must believe that He is and that He is a rewarder of those who seek Him." Paul, in Romans 14:23, unapologetically teaches us God's perspective that "whatever is not from faith is sin."

Unfortunately, for most of us, knowing this is not enough to convince us to live by faith alone. We each need daily encouragement to do the right thing for the right reasons at the right time. That is why the Bible is full of stories of real people, with real faith, in real history.

Three of those real-life testimonies come from Hebrews 11:

1.   Noah trusted God and, against all evidence and public opinion, built an ark to save humanity from God's judgement (7).
2.   Abraham trusted God and left behind all that he knew to set out on the journey to claim God's promised land (8-10).
3.   Sarah trusted God and, after 90 years of not being able to have a child, conceived a son who would inherit the promises of God (11-12).

I encourage you to open up your Bible to the book of Genesis and read these great stories of faith. These testimonies in Hebrews 11 are real stories, about real people, with real faith, in real history. The stories of these real people in these historical accounts are intended to encourage you and motivate you to live the life of faith, no matter the circumstances of your life.

Seize the moment and let your story became a real-life illustration of faith.

HEBREWS 12
FAITH SUPPLIES FAITHFULNESS!

Are you tired of running the race set before you?

We are called to run the race in Hebrews 12:1-3:

Therefore, since we have so great a cloud of witnesses surrounding us,
let us also lay aside every encumbrance and the sin which so easily
entangles us, and let us run with endurance the race that is set before us,
fixing our eyes on Jesus, the author and perfecter of faith, who for the
joy set before Him endured the cross, despising the shame, and has sat
down at the right hand of the throne of God. For consider Him who has
endured such hostility by sinners against Himself, so that you will not
grow weary and lose heart.

Did you notice the "therefore?" Did you ask yourself, "What is it there
for?"

Hebrews 12 is an action call to follow in step with the "Hall of Faith"
found in Hebrews 11. Those in the great cloud of witnesses are forever our
living testimonies of how to run the race of faithful living.

A lifetime of fidelity flows from the rich supply of faith that God gives a
person. Faith shapes your worldview because the thoughts and actions of a
person's life flow out of what each person believes about God.

Jesus was able to finish the race set before Him with joy even though
God's will for His life came with great pain and suffering. Jesus' faith
permeated all that He did. He is forever our greatest living testimony of
how to run the race of faithful living.

Seize the moment and keep your eyes on Jesus Christ, the author and
finisher of your faith. Do not grow weary and lose heart; God's faithfulness
will fuel you to the finish line. For the joy set before you, run faithfully!

HEBREWS 13
PRAYING THE BENEDICTIONS OF GOD'S WORD!

I love the ancient benedictions found in the Bible. They are powerful prayers that we can memorize and pray often. Allow me to pray over you the closing benediction of Hebrews 13:20-21:

> Now the God of peace, who brought up from the dead the great Shepherd of the sheep through the blood of the eternal covenant, even Jesus our Lord, equip you in every good thing to do His will, working in us that which is pleasing in His sight, through Jesus Christ, to whom be the glory forever and ever. Amen.

A benediction is a pronouncement of God's favor upon His people; it's a blessing. In the Old Testament, it was a formal part of the ritual life of the Jewish people. For example, from Numbers 6:24-26, "The LORD bless you, and keep you; the LORD make His face shine on you, and be gracious to you; the LORD lift up His countenance on you, and give you peace.'"

The benediction continued into the earliest churches as a pastoral practice of blessing the congregations as they gathered.

Below are two more examples that I encourage you to receive as blessings from God through His Word to you personally.

From 1 Thessalonians 5:23, "Now may the God of peace Himself sanctify you entirely; and may your spirit and soul and body be preserved complete, without blame at the coming of our Lord Jesus Christ." Amen.

From 2 Thessalonians 3:16, "Now may the Lord of peace Himself continually grant you peace in every circumstance. The Lord be with you all!" Amen.

Seize the moment and pray God's Word over other people. Powerful prayers and blessings to give to others are already given to you through the grace of God's Word.

JAMES;
1 & 2 PETER;
1, 2 & 3 JOHN;
AND JUDE

JAMES 1
GOD AS A REFINER'S FIRE!

God as a refiner's fire is a powerful image from Malachi 3:3. I love this image and, based on it, I often pray for people: Lord Jesus, please refine (insert your name here) with your unquenchable fire of holiness, removing all that is not of You and perfecting all that is of You, so that all that (insert your name here) thinks, says, and does brings You glory. Amen.

Together, let's understand the old saying, "where there is smoke, there is fire" in a new way.

Listen to James 1:2-4, "Consider it all joy, my brethren, when you encounter various trials, knowing that the testing of your faith produces endurance. And let endurance have its perfect result, so that you may be perfect and complete, lacking in nothing."

God refines us so that we reflect to the world, more and more, the presence of the One who is pure light, eternal love, and radiant holiness. This is a journey of God's love and grace because, at the end of it, God promises that you will be "lacking in nothing."

The Spirit works within you when you dedicate your life to be a living sacrifice for His glory (Romans 12:1-2).

Your desperate grip on life is broken (yet again!).

Your disillusionments on what life should provide for you burst like old wine skins (yet again!).

Your desires for something other than God are peeled back like another thin layer of an onion (and you find yourself crying, yet again!).

If you want your life to be a living sacrifice to God, never forget: where there is smoke, there is fire!

Seize the moment and let God work in you! Don't fear the fire of His love and grace. Rather, submit to His good work and learn to trust Him, yet again!

JAMES 2
THE HEARTH OF YOUR LIFE!

In the 1500s, Martin Luther championed the fundamental Christian belief that we are saved by faith alone, and he changed the modern world in the process.

James 2:18-20 focuses our minds on the importance of living the life of faith and not just saying we have faith, lest we deceive ourselves:

> But someone may well say, "You have faith and I have works; show me your faith without the works, and I will show you my faith by my works." You believe that God is one. You do well; the demons also believe, and shudder. But are you willing to recognize, you foolish fellow, that faith without works is useless?

Luther certainly did not miss this point. Listen to this wonderful teaching that has endured 500 years and informs the church's faith and practice to this day:

> Faith is a living, daring confidence in God's grace, so sure and certain that the believer would stake life itself on it a thousand times. This knowledge of and confidence in God's grace makes people glad and bold and happy in dealing with God and with all creatures. And this is the work which the Holy Spirit performs in faith. Because of it, without compulsion, a person is ready and glad to do good to everyone, to serve everyone, to suffer everything, out of love and praise to God, who has shown this grace. Thus, it is impossible to separate works from faith, quite as impossible as to separate heat and light from fire.[2]

Seize the moment and let the heat and light of your fire shine today. Faith is the source of all good works. Study and pray God's word, for that is like adding fresh wood and ample oxygen into the hearth of your life.

---

[2] Robert Kolb, Timothy J. Wengert, and Charles P. Arand, The Book of Concord: The Confessions of the Evangelical Lutheran Church (Minneapolis, MN: Fortress Press, 2000), 576.

JAMES 3
TEACHER APPRECIATION!

Who has influenced your life and way of thinking? Are you thankful and encouraging to your teachers?

James addressed a very important issue: being thankful and supportive of our teachers, because they do an impossible task for us!

James writes in James 3:1-5:

Let not many of you become teachers, my brethren, knowing that as such we will incur a stricter judgment. For we all stumble in many ways. If anyone does not stumble in what he says, he is a perfect man, able to bridle the whole body as well. Now if we put the bits into the horses' mouths so that they will obey us, we direct their entire body as well. Look at the ships also, though they are so great and are driven by strong winds, are still directed by a very small rudder wherever the inclination of the pilot desires. So also the tongue is a small part of the body, and yet it boasts of great things. See how great a forest is set aflame by such a small fire!

James is dealing with some specific issues in the local churches, not just our everyday use of our tongue although, of course, the same principles apply. However, in context here, the focus is on how there were people most likely wagging their tongues at the teachers of the local congregations. James, the overseer of the Jerusalem church (Acts 15:13-21), was telling them to get a handle on their critique and ridicule of the early church teachers because there was only one perfect teacher: Jesus.

James was calling them to submit themselves to their teachers and not disqualify them just because they were human and made mistakes. James is calling all of us to stop being a hostile, demanding crowd and to start being a peaceful, appreciative congregation. None of us are perfect!

Seize the moment and be thankful and encouraging to your teachers.

JAMES 4
OPEN HANDS, HUMBLE HEART!

Do you hold your life and your plans tightly, as with closed fists, or do you hold your life and your plans loosely, as with open hands?

James speaks into this struggle in James 4:13-15:

Come now, you who say, "Today or tomorrow we will go to such and such a city, and spend a year there and engage in business and make a profit." Yet you do not know what your life will be like tomorrow. You are just a vapor that appears for a little while and then vanishes away. Instead, you ought to say, "If the Lord wills, we will live and also do this or that."

This is our reality all the time, as so many have experienced even before the reality of the COVID-19 pandemic, whether through a medical incident, or a work accident, or a heartbreak. Life as we know it can change today.

While it is honest to say that we know this intellectually, it is also honest to acknowledge that, until we experience total loss of control in our lives, we do not really live with this posture of humility toward our lives, our plans, or our life ambitions. We keep making, and fighting for, our plans, and we assume they will happen!

We hold everything tightly—until we don't because we can't. This is when the deepest decision of our lives is made: to truly trust God, and His goodness and grace over our lives, or keep fighting for control and the ability to make life work out the way we want it to.

Did you know that this passage is an application of verse 10, when James writes, "Humble yourselves in the presence of the Lord, and He will exalt you"?

Seize the moment and open your hands to God today. He loves you and you can trust Him!

JAMES 5
JOURNEY WITH PATIENT PERSEVERANCE!

I started running again a couple of years ago. I am greatly enjoying running on the trail around Westwood Lake and on the Wilbur Wright Trail and am now working toward a trail marathon. It is amazing how much long-distance running mirrors the Christian life. Both require a patient perseverance—a long slow obedience in the same direction!

James 5:7-8 closes the letter with a call to patient perseverance, knowing that all things will bear fruit in their season: "Therefore be patient, brethren, until the coming of the Lord. The farmer waits for the precious produce of the soil, being patient about it, until it gets the early and late rains. You too be patient; strengthen your hearts, for the coming of the Lord is near."

Patience is the Fruit of the Spirit (Galatians 5:22-23) that God has given you and that He calls you to cultivate as good fruit. In fact, patient perseverance is necessary for you to become whole and holy.

You see, God wants you to become both whole and holy. Holy is being at peace with God and wholeness is being at peace with oneself. It is only when we are whole and holy that we can truly reflect the image of Christ to the world as He designed each of us to do uniquely and personally.

Cultivate the good fruit of patient perseverance in your life. I'm only 46, but the older I get the more I realize that life is a long slow obedience in the same direction. It's not a sprint, it's a marathon; more specifically, it's a trail marathon—so hit the trail today and enjoy the journey!

Seize the moment and strengthen your heart, for the coming of the Lord. Journey with patient perseverance until the finish line!

1 PETER 1
JESUS IS OUR LIVING HOPE!

Peter starts off his first letter by bursting forth in praise for who God is and what God has done for His children. In 1 Peter 1:2-5, he greets the Christians as those who are chosen,

> According to the foreknowledge of God the Father, by the sanctifying work of the Spirit, to obey Jesus Christ and be sprinkled with His blood: May grace and peace be yours in the fullest measure. Blessed be the God and Father of our Lord Jesus Christ, who according to His great mercy has caused us to be born again to a living hope through the resurrection of Jesus Christ from the dead, to obtain an inheritance which is imperishable and undefiled and will not fade away, reserved in heaven for you, who are protected by the power of God through faith for a salvation ready to be revealed in the last time.

Amen!

Peter's letter is so rich with praise to the Triune God for who He is and what He has done for His children. Peter writes, from very personal experience, how Jesus can lift people up out of the difficulties of their circumstances. In fact, Peter is writing to a church that has been scattered due to persecution.

That is why Peter calls Jesus our living hope and calls us to remember that we are made new ("born again") to Him through His resurrection. What God has given us in Jesus cannot be destroyed or diminished by life's difficulties. Peter would know this because not only did Jesus forgive him after his denials, but He also patiently persevered with Peter as he learned how to live out Christ's way of life in an ever-changing world.

Sound relevant for today? Absolutely!

Seize the moment and persevere with Jesus, our living hope today and always.

1 PETER 2
TASTE THAT THE LORD IS GOOD!

Did you know that what you think about people will determine how you interpret their words and actions?

This is such an important paradigm to understand. It is crucial that we start with our view of God, which shapes everything else we think about ourselves, the world, and other people. I'm not talking about your intellectual understanding of God, because I'm sure you've been diligent in word, but I am talking about how you relate to God beyond head knowledge—on the level of intimate knowing.

Listen to 1 Peter 2:1-3, "Therefore, putting aside all malice and all deceit and hypocrisy and envy and all slander, like newborn babies, long for the pure milk of the word, so that by it you may grow in respect to salvation, if you have tasted the kindness of the Lord."

I was reminded by a friend of a wonderful quote, "Never believe anything bad about God."

That is such a beautiful reality of how we are to view God. It shapes our worldview! As Peter commands, I am to put off all malice, deceit, hypocrisy, envy, and slander so that I can grow up in my salvation and experience the fullness of Christ's life in my life. This is wholeness and holiness; He called it the abundant life, the fullness of joy, the perfect love that drives out fear, and the peace that transcends human understanding.

These are the promises of God—and where do they start? Peter makes it very clear when he says, "if you have tasted the kindness of the Lord."

If you believe in your deepest self that God is good in all of His ways, then put aside the shadow of death and live in the love of God as the light of the world.

Seize the moment and taste that the Lord is good.

1 PETER 3
BLESSED TO SHINE!

You may have heard it said, "it doesn't amount to a hill of beans." That is an old idiom used when something, even when you sum up all the individual parts, is not worth much.

How can we be sure that our local churches, when we bring together all of the individual parts, which are the people, do amount to something of value?

At the end of the section on godly living, Peter writes in 1 Peter 3:8-9, "To sum up, all of you be harmonious, sympathetic, brotherly, kindhearted, and humble in spirit; not returning evil for evil or insult for insult, but giving a blessing instead; for you were called for the very purpose that you might inherit a blessing."

Our gathering together is valuable! We are invited to follow the example of Jesus Christ in how we treat one another. We are called to be a blessing! In fact, this is the very purpose for which you were saved and called into the family of God. Never forget that the church is composed of those people that God has called out of darkness and into His marvelous light to be the light of the world.

You probably know the children's song: this little light of mine, I'm going to let it shine. This is our inheritance—so shine the light of God! And when we all bring our little lights together and shine as one, the world will know that we are His disciples by our love for one another (John 13:35). This is one of the reasons we gather—to shine God's glory through our fellowship!

Seize the moment and remember that you have been blessed to be a blessing! Shine!

1 PETER 4
THE EFFICACY OF FAITH IS LOVE!

Right now, a lot of people are talking about the efficacy of vaccines. I actually sat through a Zoom meeting listening to an international health care expert talk about this. But, what about the efficacy of our faith in Jesus Christ?

The conversation about faith may not feel as urgent as vaccines, but it is definitely more important, as the implications are much bigger and longer lasting.

Listen to Peter explain this in 1 Peter 4:7-9, "The end of all things is near; therefore, be of sound judgment and sober spirit for the purpose of prayer. Above all, keep fervent in your love for one another, because love covers a multitude of sins. Be hospitable to one another without complaint."

Love that is given to another person in the form of forgiveness and sincere fellowship is evidence of your faith in God—we are called to forgive because our sins are forgiven! Apart from our love, there is no actual evidence of our faith. How can you say you are a Christian if you hold someone's sins against them?

Jesus, in all of His authority as the Son of God and Savior of the World, boiled down Christianity to this one commandment, from John 13:34-35: "A new commandment I give to you, that you love one another, even as I have loved you, that you also love one another. By this all men will know that you are My disciples, if you have love for one another."

John later commented on Jesus' command: "the one who loves God should love his brother also" (1 John 4:21).

Seize the moment and love people in your life by forgiving them of their sins and having sincere fellowship with them. This is what Christ first did for you!

1 PETER 5
PROMISES COME WITH PRACTICES!

Did you know that every promise of God comes with an invitation for you to put it into practice?

Listen to this as Peter closes his first letter in 1 Peter 5:6-11:

Therefore humble yourselves under the mighty hand of God, that He may exalt you at the proper time, casting all your anxiety on Him, because He cares for you. Be of sober spirit, be on the alert. Your adversary, the devil, prowls around like a roaring lion, seeking someone to devour. But resist him, firm in your faith, knowing that the same experiences of suffering are being accomplished by your brethren who are in the world. After you have suffered for a little while, the God of all grace, who called you to His eternal glory in Christ, will Himself perfect, confirm, strengthen and establish you. To Him be dominion forever and ever. Amen.

What are the promises of God in this passage?
- God has a mighty hand and will exalt you at the proper time.
- God cares about you.
- You are not alone in your suffering.
- God will perfect, confirm, strengthen, and establish you.
- God has dominion forever.

What are the corresponding invitations?
- Humble yourself and don't focus your efforts on defending or vindicating yourself.
- Cast all of your anxieties on God.
- Resist the temptation to take suffering personally.
- Persevere in God's grace through the gift of your faith.

Seize the moment and trust God, because all things for all time are in His loving hands. His promises are yours and you are invited to walk in them.

2 PETER 1
HOIST YOUR SAILS!

Have you ever watched a sailboat glide along the water using only the wind to carry it? Have you ever experienced that in your own life?

Peter speaks about God's Word in 2 Peter 1:20-21, "But know this first of all, that no prophecy of Scripture is a matter of one's own interpretation, for no prophecy was ever made by an act of human will, but men moved by the Holy Spirit spoke from God."

I am daily reading through a wonderful book called *The Handbook of Bible Promises*. In it, the authors say about this passage, "The word used for 'carried along' ['moved by' in the NAS95] was used of a ship carried along on the sea by the wind. That is how the Scriptures were written; the writers, as it were, 'hoisted their sails' to the Holy Spirit, and were 'carried along' by him, so that what they wrote was exactly what he wanted written."[3]

What a beautiful image. The New Testament authors were fully engaged in the writing process, but they were carried along by the Holy Spirit. This is how we are supposed to live our lives—with the Word of God being the rudder of our ship, setting our direction, and the Holy Spirit filling our sails to carry us along. God is the one at work in us and through us to bring about His glory.

Seize the moment and entrust your direction in life, and your pace of life, to God. Keeping your hand firmly on the rudder of God's Word, hoist your sails and allow the Holy Spirit to take you deeper into God's will.

---

[3] Mike Beaumont and Martin Manser, *The Handbook of Bible Promises*, 2020, 116.

2 PETER 2
FREEDOM IN FAITH!

There is an important invitation found in 2 Peter 2:18-19, "For speaking out arrogant words of vanity they entice by fleshly desires, by sensuality, those who barely escape from the ones who live in error, promising them freedom while they themselves are slaves of corruption; for by what a man is overcome, by this he is enslaved."

What is promising you freedom while actually seeking to enslave you?

Whose promises are you listening to? Do you subscribe to the promises of Madison Avenue, of Vanity Fair, of the Stock Market, or of Hollywood?

Here is the key phrase to hear as an invitation: "for by what a [person] is overcome, by this he [or she] is enslaved."

What has the ability to overtake you? Is it the love of the world, and all of its empty and short-sighted promises, or is it the love of God, and His great and magnificent promises?

In the previous chapter, Peter writes in verse 4, "For by these He has granted to us His precious and magnificent promises, so that by them you may become partakers of the divine nature, having escaped the corruption that is in the world by lust."

You are being invited today, whether once again or for the first time, to escape the corruption that is in the world by lust and rest in your fellowship with God through faith in Jesus Christ.

Seize the moment and pay attention to your appetites and desires. Does anything have a grip on you that is promising you more than it can deliver? Seek freedom by way of your faith in Christ!

2 PETER 3
GRACE TO YOUR NEIGHBOR!

Listen to Peter in 2 Peter 3:9, "The Lord is not slow about His promise, as some count slowness, but is patient toward you, not wishing for any to perish but for all to come to repentance."

God has promised; the Father will keep His promises to His children. God desires for all the families of the earth to be blessed with His eternal life in Heaven and with abundance in this life.

Jesus Christ was crucified, resurrected, and ascended to the right hand of the Father where today He is interceding for us until the day of His imminent return. His return is no reason to fear, but rather it is a reason to rejoice! We are to live in continual praise to God and in anticipation of His coming glory.

God desires that none should perish and has blessed us that we may be a blessing to others, so they see Christ in us and come to repentance! The beauty is that we can lose nothing that God has given us, so we can confidently give away all that God has called us to steward.

Seize the moment by bringing God's blessing of grace to all Jesus calls your neighbor. The time is short, and the harvest is plentiful. Live out of the abundance of your assurance!

1 JOHN 1
THE PROMISE OF JOY!

If you trust someone, and know their heart, it is easy to give them the benefit of the doubt, or to lovingly read between the lines on what they are saying. That is why I love reading the Bible, and especially the letters of John. His heart is beautiful, and his desire for us is so clear in all that he writes.

John expresses his motives for writing his first letter in 1 John 1:4, "These things we write, so that our joy may be made complete."

John is writing his letter to us so that we may experience the fullness of joy promised by Jesus Christ. Listen to the promise of Jesus from John 15:9-11:

Just as the Father has loved Me, I have also loved you; abide in My love. If you keep My commandments, you will abide in My love; just as I have kept My Father's commandments and abide in His love. These things I have spoken to you so that My joy may be in you, and that your joy may be made full.

Seize the moment and trust the heart of God for you and your life. Jesus wants our joy to be complete so let's obey His commands so that we may abide in His love!

1 JOHN 2
WALK LIKE JESUS!

What does it mean to follow Jesus?

There are two verses in 1 John 2 that I want to highlight because they illuminate one another and will teach us what it means to follow Jesus.

One of my favorite statements on discipleship is found in 1 John 2:5b-6, "By this we know that we are in Him: the one who says he abides in Him ought himself to walk in the same manner as He walked."

Now, couple that with the last verse of the chapter, 1 John 2:29, "If you know that He is righteous, you know that everyone also who practices righteousness is born of Him."

To follow Jesus is "to walk in the same manner as He walked," which means we are following the call to "practice righteousness." Never forget that our right relationship with God (righteousness) is possible only because we are born again through our union with Jesus Christ by grace through faith. That is the abiding relationship we have in the easy yoke of Jesus!

Seize the moment and walk as Jesus walked. We emulate Jesus, not by putting on a robe and sandals, but by living out the work of the Holy Spirit. We are to live faith, hope, and love—the theological virtues of our faith!

1 JOHN 3
A LIFE OF PRAYER BEARS FRUIT!

Remember that your life of prayer bears the good fruit of practical love! John writes in 1 John 3:16-18,

> We know love by this, that He laid down His life for us; and we ought to lay down our lives for the brethren. But whoever has the world's goods, and sees his brother in need and closes his heart against him, how does the love of God abide in him? Little children, let us not love with word or with tongue, but in deed and truth.

While I believe in and practice a disciplined life of prayer and study, the Christian life is a call to live out our faith in practical acts of sacrificial love for each another. We are to follow Jesus' example and love one another sacrificially so that the world will know that we are His disciples (John 13:34-35).

We all have our personalities and preferences, but, for Spirit-filled Christians, living out our faith is both/and—the life of prayer and study will bear the fruit of practical love!

Seize the moment and love "in deed and truth." A prayer leads to making a phone call to check on someone today, which may lead to delivering a meal, dropping off a bag of groceries, or shoveling a driveway. You don't have to do everything for everyone, just do something for someone! It starts with prayer.

1 JOHN 4
THE LOVE OF GOD!

If I was to tell you of only one thing about God, it would be the love of God! God's love illuminates my path as I seek to follow Jesus and become like Him in His easy yoke, gentle and humble in heart, fully submissive to the Father's will—only saying what He would have me say, and only doing that which He would have me do.

The love of God is an immeasurable blessing that allows me to be immersed in the eternal fellowship of the Triune God—Father, Son, and Holy Spirit—The Trinity demonstrates for us the perfect communion of faith, hope, and love.

Listen to the beloved of Jesus speak of the love of God in 1 John 4:16-19:

We have come to know and have believed the love which God has for us. God is love, and the one who abides in love abides in God, and God abides in him. By this, love is perfected with us, so that we may have confidence in the day of judgment; because as He is, so also are we in this world. There is no fear in love; but perfect love casts out fear, because fear involves punishment, and the one who fears is not perfected in love. We love, because He first loved us.

Seize the moment and allow all of your fears to be swallowed by the irresistible love of God, which has been so richly lavished upon you in Jesus Christ, crucified, risen, and coming again.

1 JOHN 5
THE UNFORCED RHYTHMS OF GRACE!

Do you feel overcome by the situations of the world? Do you feel burdened to do something about it?

We read in 1 John 5:3-4, "For this is the love of God, that we keep His commandments; and His commandments are not burdensome. For whatever is born of God overcomes the world; and this is the victory that has overcome the world—our faith."

Our faith in Jesus Christ is the victory because Jesus has already overcome the world. Never forget that our victory is vicarious—it is what Christ has done, not what we must do! We prevent ourselves from becoming overwhelmed and burdened by it all by remembering it's not us who can do anything, but anything we do is by the grace of Jesus who does the work in and through us!

We are to share in His work and partner with His power and presence in the world. This is why Jesus' invitation in Matthew 11:28-30 is so important, "Come to Me, all who are weary and heavy-laden, and I will give you rest. Take My yoke upon you and learn from Me, for I am gentle and humble in heart, and you will find rest for your souls. For My yoke is easy and My burden is light."

Seize the moment and let all your work be done in partnership with Jesus in the unforced rhythms of grace.

2 JOHN
CHOSEN CHILDREN!

I want to emphasize to you the heart of John's short letter, called 2 John; it was written from one congregation to another—from one part of the family to another.

Listen to John at the beginning of the letter in verses 4-6:

I was very glad to find some of your children walking in truth, just as we have received commandment to do from the Father. Now I ask you, lady, not as though I were writing to you a new commandment, but the one which we have had from the beginning, that we love one another. And this is love, that we walk according to His commandments. This is the commandment, just as you have heard from the beginning, that you should walk in it.

Now notice how he finishes the letter in verses 12-13, "Though I have many things to write to you, I do not want to do so with paper and ink; but I hope to come to you and speak face to face, so that your joy may be made full. The children of your chosen sister greet you."

John's letter is a masterpiece that teaches us how we should relate to one another as members of the one Church of Jesus Christ—we should see one another as fellow children of God.

His letter also emphasizes the heartbeat of Christianity—the love of God. Love is the commandment of Jesus Christ; we are to walk in love and, in doing so, find joy in God and in one another. What a beautiful life God has created for us!

Seize the moment and walk in love today, with your brothers and sisters in Christ, so that your joy may be made full.

3 JOHN
BE HOLY AND WHOLE IN EVERY RESPECT!

3 John is another short, but powerful, book of the Bible. Listen to John's opening thoughts in verses 2-4, "Beloved, I pray that in all respects you may prosper and be in good health, just as your soul prospers. For I was very glad when brethren came and testified to your truth, that is, how you are walking in truth. I have no greater joy than this, to hear of my children walking in the truth."

John is speaking of his spiritual children—those the Lord brought to Himself through John. Just as any loving father, John cares for the growth and development of these children into adulthood.

John cares about their **holiness** and their **wholeness**:

1. **John celebrates their holiness unto the Lord**—they not only testify to the truth, which means they believe right things about God and the gospel of Jesus Christ, but they also walk in the truth, which means they are living a holy lifestyle unto the Lord. We cannot simply say that we love God and His Word, we must obey God and do what Jesus commands.

2. **John cares about their wholeness.** He wants them to be healthy people as they walk with Jesus. John cares that we are healthy in all respects—emotionally and relationally, physically and socially, so that our bodies and minds prosper in step with our souls.

Seize the moment and be holy and whole—it is for this reason that God has saved you and sent you into the world to shine His light and love.

JUDE
PRAY THE PRAYERS OF THE BIBLE!

The conclusion of the short letter of Jude is one of the most beautiful benedictions in all the Scriptures.

We read in Jude 24-25, "Now to Him who is able to keep you from stumbling, and to make you stand in the presence of His glory blameless with great joy, to the only God our Savior, through Jesus Christ our Lord, be glory, majesty, dominion and authority, before all time and now and forever. Amen."

Scripture is full of these prayers of blessing. Allow me to share three more prayers from the New Testament with you today:

1. "Now the God of peace be with you all. Amen" (Romans 15:33).

2. "Now the God of peace, who brought up from the dead the great Shepherd of the sheep through the blood of the eternal covenant, even Jesus our Lord, equip you in every good thing to do His will, working in us that which is pleasing in His sight, through Jesus Christ, to whom be the glory forever and ever. Amen" (Hebrews 13:20-21).

3. "Grace to you and peace, from Him who is and who was and who is to come, and from the seven Spirits who are before His throne, and from Jesus Christ, the faithful witness, the firstborn of the dead, and the ruler of the kings of the earth. To Him who loves us and released us from our sins by His blood— and He has made us to be a kingdom, priests to His God and Father—to Him be the glory and the dominion forever and ever. Amen" (Revelation 1:4-6).

Seize the moment and pray the prayers of the Bible—you will be blessed! Pray the prayers of the Bible with and for others—you will be a blessing!

REVELATION

REVELATION 1
ALPHA AND OMEGA!

Are you walking in the promises of God?

The Revelation of John is a message from God to give His people a persevering faith and an overwhelming hope. As we face difficulties in this life, we must stand in the victory of God, upon the promises of God!

God has revealed to us in Revelation 1:7-8, "Behold, He is coming with the clouds, and every eye will see Him, even those who pierced Him; and all the tribes of the earth will mourn over Him. So it is to be. Amen. 'I am the Alpha and the Omega,' says the Lord God, 'who is and who was and who is to come, the Almighty.'"

We are invited to stand with the Victorious One as we share in His victory—this is the work of the Alpha and the Omega, who is the beginning and the end. It is done! This is the key to our victory!

Based on this, Jesus commands our fear away in verses 17b-18, "Do not be afraid; I am the first and the last, and the living One; and I was dead, and behold, I am alive forevermore, and I have the keys of death and of Hades."

Fear has once for all been swallowed by the eternal life of God! This is the love of God!

Seize the moment and walk in faith, hope, and love. This is the promise of Revelation—the promised fulfillment of God's covenant with humanity!

REVELATION 2
UNVEILING JESUS CHRIST!

What is your understanding of Jesus Christ?

Notice how Jesus is described to the first four of the seven churches of Revelation:

- To Ephesus in 2:1, Jesus is "the One who holds the seven stars in His right hand, the One who walks among the seven golden lampstands."
- To Smyrna in 2:8, Jesus is "the first and the last, who was dead, and has come to life."
- To Pergamum in 2:12, Jesus is, "the One who has the sharp two-edged sword."
- To Thyatira in 2:18, Jesus is, "the Son of God, who has eyes like a flame of fire, and His feet are like burnished bronze."

Don't skip to the later chapters of Revelation and miss out on the Revelation we receive about Jesus Christ in the first three chapters.

God has not hidden Himself from humanity, but rather He has unveiled Himself to us through Jesus Christ. We found Jesus in the Gospel accounts, the early church history book of Acts, the 13 letters of Paul, and in every book of the New Testament.

Do you know Jesus? He has made Himself known; He desires for you to know Him personally.

Seize the moment and know Jesus. He is still revealing Himself to people today. Read your Bible, memorize God's Word, and pray without ceasing.

REVELATION 3
OVERCOMERS!

Do you ever get discouraged by your circumstances?

No matter what you are going through, you can rest in the Lord and walk in His promises. You are an overcomer!

In Revelation 3, Jesus promises great things, in His messages to the last three of the seven churches, to those who walk in His promises to overcome their circumstances:

- To Sardis, Jesus says in verse 5, "He who overcomes will thus be clothed in white garments; and I will not erase his name from the book of life, and I will confess his name before My Father and before His angels."
- To Philadelphia, Jesus says in verse 12, "He who overcomes, I will make him a pillar in the temple of My God, and he will not go out from it anymore; and I will write on him the name of My God, and the name of the city of My God, the new Jerusalem, which comes down out of heaven from My God, and My new name."
- To Laodicea, Jesus says in verse 21, "He who overcomes, I will grant to him to sit down with Me on My throne, as I also overcame and sat down with My Father on His throne."

Do you trust that Jesus is who He says He is and can do what He says He'll do? Then, don't bail before the blessing!

Seize the moment and get to know Him. Learn for yourself that He is trustworthy and true. Walk in His promises so that you too can be an overcomer!

REVELATION 4
THE FEAR OF THE LORD!

The fear of the Lord is not the same kind of fear we associate with being "scared" or "worried." Rather, it reflects the reverence and awe that comes from seeing God for who He is, and not for who we make Him out to be.

When is the last time you received a fresh revelation of God?

Revelation 4 moves me to a place of reverence and awe of God. We are ushered into the throne room in verses 2-3 and 5a:

Immediately I was in the Spirit; and behold, a throne was standing in heaven, and One sitting on the throne. And He who was sitting was like a jasper stone and a sardius in appearance; and there was a rainbow around the throne, like an emerald in appearance. Out from the throne come flashes of lightning and sounds and peals of thunder.

As the description continues, it invites us deeper. From verses 8-9, the scene unfolds around the throne as scripture describes "four living creatures, each one of them having six wings, are full of eyes around and within; and day and night they do not cease to say, 'Holy, holy, holy, is the LORD God, the Almighty, who was and who is and who is to come.'"

What an exalted view of God as He sits on His throne, with the four living beings in continual worship, and as we also read in this chapter, twenty-four elders casting their crowns in absolute surrender to God because of who He is and what He has done. They proclaim in verse 11, "Worthy are You, our Lord and our God, to receive glory and honor and power; for You created all things, and because of Your will they existed, and were created." Amen!

Seize the moment and worship Jesus Christ alone with your life. Only He is worthy!

REVELATION 5
THE WITNESSES OF JESUS' WORTHINESS!

How many witnesses are needed to determine if a matter is true?

Revelation 5 is a powerful witness to the worthiness of Jesus Christ. I pulled three quotes, just out of this one chapter, that attest to who Jesus Christ is and how worthy He is of our worship.

First, the four living creatures and twenty-four elders sang a new song, saying in verses 9-10, "Worthy are You to take the book and to break its seals; for You were slain, and purchased for God with Your blood men from every tribe and tongue and people and nation. You have made them to be a kingdom and priests to our God; and they will reign upon the earth."

Second, the angels, numbering too many to count ("myriads of myriads and thousands of thousands") said with a loud voice in verse 12, "Worthy is the Lamb that was slain to receive power and riches and wisdom and might and honor and glory and blessing."

We hear a final testimony in verse 13, "And every created thing which is in heaven and on the earth and under the earth and on the sea, and all things in them, I heard saying, 'To Him who sits on the throne, and to the Lamb, be blessing and honor and glory and dominion forever and ever.'"

Jesus is worthy to be worshipped! That is beyond a reasonable doubt.

How are you responding to these eyewitness testimonials?

Seize the moment and worship Jesus. Trust Him as your Lord and Savior. He is worthy!

REVELATION 6
GOD'S PATIENCE LEADS TO REPENTANCE!

What do the Four Horsemen of the Apocalypse and the Scroll's Seven Seals of Justice have to do with your life today? That is a good question as we look at Revelation 6.

The answer to today's opening question is two important words: Patience and repentance.

The first word describes God: **God is patient!**

In Revelation 6:10-11, the martyrs of the faith cry out to God in a loud voice,

"How long, O Lord, holy and true, will You refrain from judging and avenging our blood on those who dwell on the earth?" And there was given to each of them a white robe; and they were told that they should rest for a little while longer, until the number of their fellow servants and their brethren who were to be killed even as they had been, would be completed also.

The Bible also explains God's patience in 2 Peter 3:9, "The Lord is not slow about His promise, as some count slowness, but is patient toward you, not wishing for any to perish but for all to come to repentance."

There is our second word: **God's patience leads us to repentance!**

The purpose of Revelation is not to put God's destructive power on display, but rather it exists to exhibit God's saving power—it's not about wrath, it's about love! God is patiently calling people back to a relationship with Him!

Seize the moment and respond to God's saving power today by trusting Jesus with your past successes and failures, your present hopes and dreams, and your future questions and unknowns. God is patient with us beyond measure; our responsibility is to repent!

REVELATION 7
THE CALL OF EVANGELISM!

Does your faith have borders? Do you restrict the love of God? Who is your neighbor? Visualize this glimpse of God's Heavenly Kingdom from Revelation 7:9-10:

> After these things I looked, and behold, a great multitude which no one could count, from every nation and all tribes and peoples and tongues, standing before the throne and before the Lamb, clothed in white robes, and palm branches were in their hands; and they cry out with a loud voice, saying, "Salvation to our God who sits on the throne, and to the Lamb."

The Kingdom of God goes beyond borders! What borders need to come down in your mind, heart, and lifestyle so that you are not limiting the gospel of Jesus Christ?

Here are just a few of the common borders that people have:

National Citizenship	Political Ideology	Religion
Socioeconomic Status	Language	Gender
Education Level	Marital Status	Age
Racial Identity	Music Preferences	Attire
Ethnic Background	Generational Preferences	
Theological Orientation	Denominational Affiliation	
Technology Access, Use, and Reference		

Seize the moment as a citizen of Heaven and cross the borders so that you can reach the very people God is calling through the gospel of Jesus Christ. This is the call of evangelism; as the world comes closer though technology, the global mission field is now local—it is "glocal!"

REVELATION 8
ETERNAL PRAYERS!

Is there anything you can invest your time in today that is guaranteed to last forever?

Listen to Revelation 8:1-4:

When the Lamb broke the seventh seal, there was silence in heaven for about half an hour. And I saw the seven angels who stand before God, and seven trumpets were given to them. Another angel came and stood at the altar, holding a golden censer; and much incense was given to him, so that he might add it to the prayers of all the saints on the golden altar which was before the throne. And the smoke of the incense, with the prayers of the saints, went up before God out of the angel's hand.

In Heaven, the prayers of God's people go up before God. This same truth is also referenced in Revelation 5:8, where we see the "prayers of the saints" in "golden bowls full of incense."

Your prayers, lifted up to God, last forever! Take time today to invest yourself, your time, and your energy in eternity.

As you read the rest of Revelation 8, you will be confronted with how so many other things we invest ourselves in just won't matter at the end of the age. So much of what we get caught up in will be long gone, but our prayers lifted up to God will still be like incense to God in the throne room of Heaven.

Seize the moment and praise God today. Share with God what is on your heart, submit yourself to His purposes for your life, ask Him to lead you, and then listen for His guidance. May the God of all love and grace guide your steps through His Word and Spirit.

REVELATION 9
GOD MEETS PEOPLE AT THE BOTTOM!

When I read the judgments of God found in the Revelation of John, my heart breaks for people. Not in a prideful, "I'm better than you" kind of way, but sincerely, and with empathy. My heart breaks because I know what it is like to resist God and to keep putting my trust in myself to go where I want to go. I get it. I've been there and I've done that.

Revelation 9 is a stirring chapter. After the woes of God are released upon the Earth, and one-third of the population is killed, people are still unwilling to repent and turn to God. We read in Revelation 9:20-21:

> The rest of mankind, who were not killed by these plagues, did not repent of the works of their hands, so as not to worship demons, and the idols of gold and of silver and of brass and of stone and of wood, which can neither see nor hear nor walk; and they did not repent of their murders nor of their sorceries nor of their immorality nor of their thefts.

What does it take to get people's attention so that they will turn to God?

How low do you have to go? How low does our culture have to get?

Seize the moment and put your trust in God today. Remember, God specializes in meeting people right where they are! God meets people at the bottom of any pit! If you find yourself feeling like you, or a loved one, is hitting bottom, there is hope—His name is Jesus! Turn to Him today and He'll lift you up!

REVELATION 10
EMBRACE THE MYSTERY!

When I read Revelation 10, and John is writing down how God is revealing hidden things to us verse after verse, I am taking it all in. Just like any good mystery, God doesn't allow us to see everything up front.

Listen to Revelation 10:4, "When the seven peals of thunder had spoken, I was about to write; and I heard a voice from heaven saying, 'Seal up the things which the seven peals of thunder have spoken and do not write them.'"

How do you handle that? In the midst of God pulling back the veil through John and giving us the book of Revelation, God essentially tells us, "Not this! Now is not the time for you to know everything."

Are you OK with the fact that there are some things you are not allowed to know, yet?

Personally, I love it! I embrace the reality of the mystery of God. I love that He knows and I don't. It keeps me fully submitted, fully anticipating, and fully engaged.

Fully submitted is the life of FAITH!

Fully anticipating is the life of HOPE!

Fully engaged is the life of LOVE!

Faith, hope and love are the three theological virtues. The reality of mystery leads me to stay humble and live my life in reflection to who God is and what God is doing. And that is the life that God wants me to live.

How are you embracing the mysteries of God?

Seize the moment and live the life of faith, hope, and love.

REVELATION 11
WITNESSES TO A DARK WORLD!

What happens when you turn on a bright light in a dark room? It's shocking!

As the end nears, and the coming of Christ approaches, God will press upon His people to be the witnesses who shine brightly in the darkening days. Just as God does not leave the world without witnesses today, so God will not leave the world without witnesses in the great tribulations that are to come.

God reveals to John in Revelation 11:3-4, "'And I will grant authority to my two witnesses, and they will prophesy for twelve hundred and sixty days, clothed in sackcloth.' These are the two olive trees and the two lampstands that stand before the Lord of the earth."

Just like the two heavenly witnesses, you too have been granted great authority as God's witness to the gospel of Jesus Christ. God has enlightened you through the gift of faith, and He has empowered you with the indwelling of the Holy Spirit. God has called you to bear great spiritual fruit so that all may see His transforming power in and through you.

You are an ambassador of Jesus Christ. You were saved to shine His light to all who are caught in the darkness of these last days. Don't be surprised when people are shocked by you and your faith! That's what light does in dark places.

Seize the moment and shine as a witness for Christ in these dark days!

REVELATION 12
JESUS' REIGN IS WITH A ROD OF IRON!

What does it mean when someone rules with a rod of iron?

Revelation 12:5 describes the rule of Jesus Christ in the Kingdom of God, "And she gave birth to a son, a male child, who is to rule all the nations with a rod of iron; and her child was caught up to God and to His throne."

It is also used in Revelation 2:26-27; 19:15; and Psalm 2:9.

Contemporary dictionaries define it like this, "to control or govern very strictly or harshly." The connotations are negative, tyrannical even, but the Bible is using it in a positive way.

To rule with a "rod of iron" means that Jesus' reign will be an "unyieldingly just reign." His rule over people will show no favoritism. He will not deviate from justice to allow any perversion or distortion of what is right and true. He will rule according to the standards established by God for His creation.

That is not tyranny. That is not harsh. That is love!

The intent of this image for the future is to invoke hope in the people of God. The goal is to inspire faithfulness until that day. Though we currently live in a world where justice is not always consistent, and government is not always for the people, we can anticipate what is to come. We can live today with great expectation of all things being made right and true.

Seize the moment and face the injustices of today with faith, hope, and love because what God has promised for tomorrow is right and true.

REVELATION 13
PERSEVERE IN YOUR FAITH!

Have you ever felt like you "missed the forest for the trees"?

I remember flying in a military helicopter over the mountains of Dahlonega, Georgia during the second phase of the US Army Ranger School. As a 1997 graduate of this prestigious training, I spent a lot of time out in those mountains, but they were never so beautiful as when I was up in the helicopter flying over them instead of trudging through them. I was so exhausted by my circumstances and so focused on the task at hand that I could not see the beauty that surrounded me—I lost sight of the forest for the trees!

I am returning to the Dahlonega area in 2021, 24 years later, to hike the section of the Appalachian Trail that starts at Springer Mountain and meanders through those same ridge lines around Dahlonega. Though the terrain will not have changed, I guarantee my perspective will be different! I'm excited to see to the forest!

Revelation 13 is an overwhelming chapter describing the two beasts, the anti-Christ and his prophet, but verse 10b gives us an important perspective: "Here is the perseverance and the faith of the saints."

But for this one small clause in the middle verse of this daunting chapter, the temptation would be to give in to fear. John is saying to us, the readers of Revelation, "don't lose the forest for the trees." Perspective changes everything—God has a bigger plan than what we can see, so don't let the details of today or the fears of tomorrow distract you from your faith.

Seize the moment and persevere in your faith! Don't lose sight of the forest for the trees!

REVELATION 14
LEGACY OF GOOD WORKS!

What is your life's legacy?

Revelation 14:12-13 calls us to persevere in good works:

Here is the perseverance of the saints who keep the commandments of God and their faith in Jesus. And I heard a voice from heaven, saying, "Write, 'Blessed are the dead who die in the Lord from now on!'" "Yes," says the Spirit, "so that they may rest from their labors, for their deeds follow with them."

This is the first time the Holy Spirit explicitly speaks in the Revelation of John, and it is to those who are in union with Jesus, or, as I like to say, are in the yoke of Jesus. There is a blessing for them; the second of the seven beatitudes (blessings) of Revelation, reminiscent of Jesus' beatitudes in the Sermon on the Mount: they will leave a legacy of faith.

In the easy yoke of Jesus Christ, you will fulfill the purpose of your life by producing the good works God has prepared for you to do in your life. Ephesians 2:10 teaches us God's promise of good works "For we are His workmanship, created in Christ Jesus for good works, which God prepared beforehand so that we would walk in them."

Seize the moment and focus on your union with Jesus. The good works that are done while in the easy yoke of Jesus are promised to follow after you!

REVELATION 15
A MAGNIFICENT VISTA OF GOD'S JUDGMENT!

Have you ever stood on the edge of the Grand Canyon or on the top of Clingman's Dome and found yourself awestruck by the scene set before you?

Revelation 15 shows us a vista of God's mighty judgments. Listen to the praise and worship of the angelic watchers as they witness the majesty of God who sits upon the throne in verses 3-4:

And they sang the song of Moses, the bond-servant of God, and the song of the Lamb, saying, "Great and marvelous are Your works, O Lord God, the Almighty; Righteous and true are Your ways, King of the nations! Who will not fear, O Lord, and glorify Your name? For You alone are holy; For all the nations will come and worship before you, for your righteous acts have been revealed."

The angels' response to God's judgment of sin is praise and adoration. What is your response?

God loves you and wants only the best for you! Do you believe this about God and His judgment?

God knows that sin is not good for you, even when you think that what you are doing is best for you. It is our limited understanding of God that causes us to rebel against God's best for our lives.

This is why we must make it our greatest ambition to know God. In knowing God, we will find ourselves in the loving embrace of a good Father who desires to put His name on us and shine His glory through us.

Seize the moment and worship God in truth and spirit! Fear not, for the Lord is with you and desires good for you and for all of His creation.

REVELATION 16
GOD IS THE TRUE AND RIGHTEOUS JUDGE!

Are you quick to judge others?

Notice what the angel proclaims in the midst of God pouring out His wrath upon the Earth. From Revelation 16:5–7:

> And I heard the angel of the waters saying, "Righteous are You, who are and who were, O Holy One, because You judged these things; for they poured out the blood of saints and prophets, and You have given them blood to drink. They deserve it." And I heard the altar saying, "Yes, O Lord God, the Almighty, true and righteous are Your judgments."

Don't be too quick to dish out what you think another person deserves; Jesus is the only righteous Judge. Jesus warns us of this in Matthew 7:2: "For in the way you judge, you will be judged; and by your standard of measure, it will be measured to you."

Take a deep breath and remember this before you judge another person. It's like a boomerang!

God has good reasons for His judgements. They are not only justice, but they are mercy. Listen to God's yearning for those who are facing His judgment in Revelation 16:9, "Men were scorched with fierce heat; and they blasphemed the name of God who has the power over these plagues, and they did not repent so as to give Him glory."

God does not desire for any to perish but wants all to repent and come to a saving faith in Him (2 Peter 3:9).

Seize the moment and learn to read all of God's Word through the lens of who God is and not through the lens of your own anger with others or your angst with the world's situations. He is sovereign. He is good. He is just. His judgments are always righteous and true.

REVELATION 17
THE VICTORY OF THE LAMB OF GOD!

Will good ever prevail over evil?

This question is at the heart of every great epic story! This question is answered by the gospel of Jesus Christ!

In Revelation 17 we see the forces of evil aligned against God, but we have this assurance found in verse 14, "These will wage war against the Lamb, and the Lamb will overcome them, because He is Lord of lords and King of kings, and those who are with Him are the called and chosen and faithful."

Jesus is Lord of lords and King of kings! That is who He is and because He is preeminent over all things, there is nothing in this life or the next that can defeat Him or separate you from His love. As Paul said in Romans 8:37-39:

But in all these things we overwhelmingly conquer through Him who loved us. For I am convinced that neither death, nor life, nor angels, nor principalities, nor things present, nor things to come, nor powers, nor height, nor depth, nor any other created thing, will be able to separate us from the love of God, which is in Christ Jesus our Lord.

This is the promise of your security! The victory of Jesus Christ, won once and for all on the Cross of Calvary has defeated the forces of evil, has removed the sting of death, and has loosened the grip of sin forever.

I started by asking the question: Will good ever prevail over evil? The answer is: "It is finished!"

Seize the moment and walk in the victory that has been won for you, guaranteed by the sovereign grace of the Lamb of God.

REVELATION 18
IN A SINGLE HOUR!

Where is your hope and security?

For many, it is in things that can be taken from them in a single hour. Three times in Revelation 18, we are warned not to put our hope and security in what can be taken away from us so easily:

· "Woe, woe, the great city, Babylon, the strong city! For in one hour your judgment has come" (10).
· "Woe, woe, the great city, she who was clothed in fine linen and purple and scarlet, and adorned with gold and precious stones and pearls; for in one hour such great wealth has been laid waste" (16-17a)!
· 'Woe, woe, the great city, in which all who had ships at sea became rich by her wealth, for in one hour she has been laid waste' (19)!

It strikes me that much of human accomplishment that takes years, even generations, to build can be destroyed, or taken away, in a single hour. This is true not only for our lives, but it is also true for our communities and nations.

So, I ask again, where is your hope and security?

Thanks be to God for sending His one and only Son, Jesus Christ, the Indescribable Gift, who has made a way for people to give their lives to something that cannot be taken away in a single hour!

Seize the moment and invest your time and resources into a kingdom that is not of this world—one that cannot be taken away in a single hour. You will never be disappointed when you give generously to the work of the Lord Jesus Christ.

REVELATION 19
HALLELUJAH!

Have you ever heard someone shout out, "Hallelujah," and did you wonder what it meant?

Hallelujah is a Hebrew word transliterated into the Greek of the New Testament and then used by people all around the world, regardless of their native language.

The word Hallelujah is found four times in Revelation 19 (1, 3, 4, and 6). Ready to be surprised? These are the only four usages of this word in the New Testament. I found that hard to believe because it feels like a more common word, so I did a word study and found it to be true.

What does Hallelujah mean? In the Hebrew, it literally means Praise Jah (a shortening of Yahweh)! When we use it, we are saying, "Praise God!"

In Revelation 19, this word of praise is coming from the great multitude, the twenty-four elders, and the four living creatures. It is used to praise God for who He is (1, 4, and 6), for what He has done (1 and 3), and for what He will do (6).

How are we to use the word Hallelujah in our lives today?

First, when we want to praise God for who He is and lift up His name! When you meditate upon who God is, you will not be able to do anything but praise Him.

Second, we use Hallelujah to praise God for His mighty works. The heavenly parties did this when they praised God for what He had done: His righteous and just judgment on Babylon (Revelation 19:1-6). They also praised God for what He would do: the marriage of the Lamb with the Bride, which is biblical imagery that the completion of all things (*eschatos*) would forever and perfectly unite Jesus and His Church (Revelation 19:6ff).

Seize the moment and cry out Hallelujah with your life. May your words and actions praise the Sovereign God for who He is and all He does to bring His glory from Heaven to Earth.

REVELATION 20
THE END OF THE BEGINNING!

Do you know your place in God's ongoing story?

Revelation 20 is the end of the beginning—and the best is yet to come!

When I teach a survey class of the Bible, I take time to explain how Genesis 1-11 serves as the prologue, and Revelation 4-22 serves as the epilogue, to the greatest story ever told. I encourage you to take some time to read the prologue and epilogue of the Bible and see the whole Bible as one epic story.

Both are essential to understanding the meta-narrative of God's redemptive story. Chapter 1 would be the choosing of God's people, beginning with Abraham in Genesis 12, and the final chapter ends with Jesus Christ's final words to the seven churches, who are the descendants of Abraham, in Revelation 1-3. Just as the Genesis prologue sets the stage and introduces God as the main character, the Revelation epilogue shows that the story does not end in this age of the Church.

While we currently live in the age of the Church; this age of grace concludes with the imminent return of Jesus Christ, who will come as the conquering King to vanquish evil, rule the nations, and judge the deeds of humanity.

Until these days are completed, and evil is vanquished with all sin judged (the emphasis of Revelation 20), we must walk through hardship and remain faithful.

Faithful are those whose names are written in the Book of Life. Faithful are those who do not take the mark of the beast. Faithful are those who will never taste of the second death, the lake of fire.

Seize the moment and take your place in God's story. Finish faithfully until the One who promises returns, makes all things new, and begins the next part of the story.

REVELATION 21
HOLD ON TO YOUR FAITH!

The Bible ends with a triumphant view of God's reign over His creation. There is hope! There is an end to all things, which truly reveals the power and awesomeness of God! There is a fulfillment to the promise, which is greater than our temporary sufferings upon this Earth as we live by faith and not by sight.

My response to God's vision of the New Heaven and New Earth is that we need to hold on because the best is yet to come!

Revelation 21:22–27 teaches us about the New Heaven and New Earth:

I saw no temple in it, for the Lord God the Almighty and the Lamb are its temple. And the city has no need of the sun or of the moon to shine on it, for the glory of God has illumined it, and its lamp is the Lamb. The nations will walk by its light, and the kings of the earth will bring their glory into it. In the daytime (for there will be no night there) its gates will never be closed; and they will bring the glory and the honor of the nations into it; and nothing unclean, and no one who practices abomination and lying, shall ever come into it, but only those whose names are written in the Lamb's book of life.

Seize the moment and hold on to your faith as you live day-by-day. As Jesus so triumphantly declares in Revelation 21:5-6, "Behold, I am making all things new ... It is done!" It will be done as God promised, so hold on! You may not be able to see it yet, but put your faith in the One who promises—He is faithful and true!

REVELATION 22
YOU ARE BLESSED!

You have God's favor—you are "blessed!"

How?

Just as Jesus taught about God's blessings in the beatitudes of the Sermon on the Mount (Matthew 5:3-11), so we now finish with the beatitudes of the Revelation of John. Unlike Jesus' sermon where the beatitudes come in rapid succession, these beatitudes are found from the beginning to the end of the book of Revelation, with the last two being in this concluding chapter.

Listen to the last two from Revelation 22:7, "And behold, I am coming quickly. Blessed is he who heeds the words of the prophecy of this book." And Revelation 22:14, "Blessed are those who wash their robes, so that they may have the right to the tree of life, and may enter by the gates into the city."

You are blessed! This is the good fruit of abiding in the Word! As you have disciplined your life for godliness and have sincerely read God's Word with the motive to listen and obey, the result will be that you are blessed.

I encourage you to read the first and sixth beatitudes, found in Revelation 1:3 and 22:7, as the bookends of the book of Revelation and press into God's promise in this last book of the Bible. As Revelation 1:3 promises, "Blessed is he who reads and those who hear the words of the prophecy, and heed the things which are written in it; for the time is near."

You are blessed when you remain pure from the defilements of this world and anticipate the promises of eternity awaiting you at the finish line of this race set before you (these promises are in the other five beatitudes found in Revelation 14:13; 16:15; 19:9; 20:6; and 22:14).

Seize the moment and finish the race set before you. You have everything you need to be "Blessed!" Don't bail before the blessing!

AFTERWORD

Thank you for taking the time to read *Seize the Moment*. Whether you utilized this book as a personal daily devotional book, or as a pastoral sermon-starter resource, I am humbled and thankful that you invested time to read it.

This book was birthed in the trenches of pastoral work in the local church. The journey that this book represents required great partnership within a congregation and a daily commitment of a local church pastor to walk closely with Jesus through one of the most demanding and exhausting experiences of the twenty-first century American church. Both the congregational partnership and the pastoral priority are essential to the missional success of any church. What started as one local church's very intentional leadership response to the COVID-19 pandemic in March 2020 has transformed into an essential daily tool to focus the congregation on the urgency and importance of prioritizing their spiritual formation.

Seize the Moment is not a program; rather, it is a rhythm of life for both the pastor and the congregation that focuses all of us on the one thing that is necessary—sitting at the feet of Jesus and listening to His Word (Luke 10:42). There is no greater work of pastoral ministry than to focus God's people on the strengthening of their spiritual vitality through a real relationship with Jesus Christ, modeled by pastors and leaders themselves. The daily discipline of the pastor to read God's Word, prayerfully study it, and listen intently for God to give the pastor a timely and accurate word for the congregation has always been a critical task of the pastor in a local church. *Seize the Moment* has taken that task to the next level by facilitating a daily practice of feeding the congregation a fresh word from God, through the pastor, to the congregation. Every pastor knows that a weekly sermon is not enough, but very few pastors have taken practical steps to remedy the deficiency of that model. I have found a way as a pastor to provide six days per week of quality discipleship material without overcommitting myself or burdening the congregation, and I hope this rhythm of life inspires other pastors to do something similar for their congregations. I can attest it has been a blessing to me, and I find the yoke easy and the burden light because it was birthed by the Spirit for a time such as this.

This timely and relevant work has become the essential daily discipline of my pastoral ministry to the congregation of First Baptist Church, but it also has become the heartbeat of how we prioritize our church's ministry regarding the spiritual formation of every member of the congregation. Every person who receives this daily devotion is invited to read God's Word systematically along with the pastor and prayerfully reflect upon how they are being invited to apply God's Word to their own lives. *Seize the Moment* is more than a daily devotional; it is an invitation into an effective spiritual formation journey, and it is one the pastor and congregation answer together.

While the COVID-19 pandemic was the impetus of this great effort to communicate daily with the congregation and provide them with quality biblical content, the ongoing initiative known as *Seize the Moment* is now a daily congregational resource to provide structure for the keystone habits of daily spiritual reading (one chapter per day from the Bible), the meditation upon a specific section of that chapter (a devotion based on that same chapter), and the prayerful listening to how the Holy Spirit would have the reader seize the moment to the glory of God that day (apply God's Word to your life in this timely and relevant way).

I praise God for this unexpected blessing in my life, for my pastoral ministry, and for the congregational health of our faith community. May God lead you into the same benefits and blessings of a vibrant daily relationship with Jesus Christ. All glory to God!

ABOUT THE AUTHOR

Jerry D. Ingalls serves as the Lead Pastor of First Baptist Church of New Castle, Indiana. He is an ordained minister and has been serving ABC-USA churches in pastoral ministry since 2003. Prior to serving in pastoral ministry, Jerry honorably served in the US Army as an Infantry Officer with assignments in the 82nd Airborne Division and the US Army's World Class Athlete Program, earning awards such as the US Army Ranger Tab, Airborne Wings, Air Assault Wings, and the Expert Infantryman Badge. Additionally, Jerry served as a Chaplain Candidate and graduated from the US Army Chaplain School (2007). He has earned a Doctor of Ministry (DMin) in Pastoral Studies from Grace Theological Seminary (2020), a Master of Divinity (MDiv) from Fuller Theological Seminary (2008), an MS in Counseling and Student Development from the C.W. Post Campus of Long Island University (2000), and a BS in Psychological Engineering from the United States Military Academy at West Point (1996). Jerry was a 1996 Academic All-American athlete at West Point and still holds the Academy and Patriot League records in the hammer throw. He married Kimberly in 1999 and by God's grace they have been blessed with three wonderful children—Beorn, Alana, and Willow. Jerry enjoys reading with his children, camping with his family, backcountry hiking, trail running, and competing at the master's level in track and field.

AGF PUBLISHING, LLC

We publish books and media in an array of genres, always aiming to entertain, educate, inform, and inspire people of all ages and reading levels. We encourage and train writers from all backgrounds to work with us in bringing their stories and knowledge to a worldwide audience.

Learn more about the company and all of its offerings at www.agfpublishingcompany.com

NORTHSIDE BOOKS & MEDIA
AN AGF PUBLISHING IMPRINT

Northside Books & Media encourages and equips Christians worldwide through fiction and nonfiction. Look for more titles, author information and call for manuscripts at

https://agfpublishingcompany.com/northside-books-media/

Made in United States
Orlando, FL
02 December 2021

11077170R00165